MELANCHTHON:
ALIEN OR ALLY?

CAMBRIDGE
UNIVERSITY PRESS
LONDON: BENTLEY HOUSE
NEW YORK   TORONTO   BOMBAY
CALCUTTA MADRAS: MACMILLAN

MELANCHTHON: ALIEN OR ALLY?

BY

FRANZ HILDEBRANDT

LIC. THEOL. (BERLIN), PH.D. (CANTAB.)

PASTOR AND LECTURER IN CAMBRIDGE

CAMBRIDGE

AT THE UNIVERSITY PRESS

1946

To

MY MOTHER

PRINTED IN GREAT BRITAIN AT THE
UNIVERSITY PRESS, CAMBRIDGE

CONTENTS

AUTHOR'S NOTE

Melanchthon's works have been quoted from the *Corpus Reformatorum*, ed. Bredschneider (*CR*); Luther's from the Weimarer Ausgabe (*WA*; the table-talks, Tischreden: *WA Ti*), in a few instances from Walch and the Erlanger Ausgabe (*EA*), his letters from De Wette's edition and his disputations from Drews. The Lutheran Confessions of Faith have been quoted from J. T. Müller's edition (Gütersloh, 1928); they contain, besides the three oecumenical symbols, the *Augsburg Confession* and *Apologia*, Luther's *Articuli Smalcaldici* (with Melanchthon's *Tractatus de Potestate ac Primatu Papae*), his *Minor* and *Major Catechisms*, and the *Formula Concordiae*. For Wesley's Works the 14-volume edition (London, 1829–31) has been used. Nearly all German and many Latin quotations, which my mother and my friend Dr Werner Simonson readily helped to copy out, have been translated, except for the footnotes, but without Latin altogether and a few words of Greek Melanchthon could not speak. Similarly, where Luther, in his typical manner, combines German and Latin in the same sentence, the Latin has usually been retained. After a revision, which owes much to the kindly advice of Professor C. H. Dodd, it is hoped that the languages are mixed in fair proportion, that students will not be left with too many allusions, and that experts will forgive the author where he has been too elementary.

INTRODUCTION

Cambridge once hoped for Melanchthon to become Regius Professor in the Divinity Faculty; the hope never materialized, but it is still true to say that there is something in the atmosphere of our University which invites at any rate the study of this man. Had he only had the vision and the courage to make the long journey across the Channel, and, as the historian will remind us, had it only been at a different moment and under a different regime, he might well have found here the fulfilment of the 'vita in otio literario' which was the secret ideal of his heart,[1] and he would have been delivered from the *rabies theologorum* which even then was the typical disease of the continent. However—be that as it may—the traveller who has left the Third Reich behind and walks for the first time through King's or Clare towards the University Library cannot help feeling both drunk at the taste of freedom and overwhelmed by the unbroken unity of medieval tradition and modern life; and sick as he is of dictatorship in politics *and* in theology, of 'secular despair' *and* of 'Christian realism', he longs more than ever for 'true humanism', and he turns to Melanchthon. Of course, the humanists have always been more popular in England than the Reformers; it is impossible to imagine that at any time Luther could have occupied the chair of Erasmus at Queens'; but it is safe to assume a special sympathy for the man who in many respects stands half-way between them, the humanist among the Reformers, the mediator in all controversies, the well-tempered scholar and diplomat who lacks all the features which are so repellent in the rustic face of Luther.

Needless to say, the very fact that he appeals to Englishmen makes him all the more suspect in the eyes of contemporary continental theologians. Is it not time, they will ask, to preach

[1] 'Cupiebam κἄν τρόπον ἀπανθρωπότερον vitam in otio literario degere inter sacra silentia τῆς φιλοσοφίας, ὅτι τοῦτο ἥδιστόν ἐστι καλοῖς, ut Plato ait. Verum quando id per fortunam nondum licet, βιωτέον, ὡς δυνάμεθα, οὐχ ὡς θελόμεθα, sequamur plausum hominum et istam popularem aleam', *CR*, 1, 32. 'Saepe mihi venit in mentem illud quod scribit Aeschines ad quendam amicum, gaudere se quod a Reipublicae administratione liberatus sit, perinde ac si a rabiosa cane liberatus esset. Ita ego non aegre feram rumpi aliquando has compedes, quibus hactenus vinctus hic teneor. Nam quod reliquum est aetatis, totum cupio conferre ad excitanda litterarum studia, quantum omnino omnibus animi atque ingenii nervis ac viribus contendere possum', 3, 420.

Luther to the British? to make them see at last the final break
between Reformation and Humanism? to teach them the lessons
of the German Church struggle? to welcome and strengthen that
minority which is just beginning to move 'on to orthodoxy'?
No doubt there is a need and a place for all this: the need is for
the Church militant and the place is the pulpit, and it is here that
'Barthianism' will make its contribution and its conquests in the
younger generation. Arrogant as it must sound, there are many
voices in the chorus of the 'post-anti-liberals' which sing precisely
the notes heard on the continent in the 1920's, and that may well
be a necessary crisis through which each country has to pass in
turn. But when all is said that can be said in condemnation of
'Anglo-Saxon' preaching, the question remains: what of the
future? What after the schoolmaster has spoken his final word?
What after the last 1000 pages volume of correct reformed
'Dogmatik' (if there ever is to be a last one) will have appeared?
Theology cannot live on repetitions; and while for the evangelist
Philippians iii, 1 is vitally true, the teacher must inevitably become
tired of telling the story of the German Confessional Church and
begin to wonder whether after all there is not something which
we continentals may profitably learn from the other side.

It is this aspect with which we are concerned here. The task
is admittedly not evangelistic, not of primary importance in the
sense of being vital for the immediate 'war effort' of the Church
in its many persecutions; nevertheless, it is essential, for it is
reconstructive. Whatever we may think of the English pulpit at
the present time, the English University can only be the object
of our envy; and its superiority lies in that conception of an
'universitas' of art and science which on the continent has
largely been lost or willingly been given up. We may boast
of having further advanced in the world of the twentieth century;
but the 'myth' of this century is pagan, its 'education' is for
death, its 'revolution' is nihilism. With all our radicalism we have
come so fatally near to barbarism that only another world war
could open our eyes to the value in the tradition of those other
nineteen centuries on which our Western civilization is built;
now that the foundations are threatened we feel that we must defend
them or perish, and we begin to understand the meaning of the
ancient universities, the symbolism of the fact that they still stand
unbroken and untouched. Let us be honest and realize that we
cannot jump over our own shadow, returning to our grandfathers

while denying our fathers; we cannot have the sixteenth century
without the eighteenth and nineteenth just as we cannot cultivate
Bach and Reger while shutting our ears to Beethoven. However
violently we may dislike and resent it, we are children both of
the reformers and of the humanists; their combined influence has
shaped our modern thinking more than anything else; and to find
the right proportion between the two is the cardinal problem of
all sound learning which Melanchthon, the 'praeceptor Ger-
maniae', was the first to face.

But to follow his footsteps is to tread a dangerous path. It is
to counteract the purist tendency of modern Protestant theology,
which has taught us ever more carefully to analyse and eliminate
all humanist elements from the pure doctrine of the Reformation
and which even now is trying to clear Luther and Calvin themselves from the rudiments of 'natural revelation'. We shall constantly run the risk of the Anathema from Basle or similar authoritative quarters, and it would be foolish to overlook the warning
against the abyss of heresies into which the humanist of all times
and types is likely to fall. But it would be no less foolish to allow
ourselves to be frightened into a kind of isolationism which makes
theology the business of training colleges and abandons its position in the 'universitas literarum'. The confessor is greater than
the professor, the role of Luther more gratifying than that of
Melanchthon; yet the Reformation could not have been carried
through without the help of the latter, and what we want to know is
just to what extent the fathers of our Church availed themselves of
the services of the humanist ancilla. It is not so much a question
of coordination or synthesis between two equal partners but
rather one of engaging domestic help at the moment and in the
interest of the 'establishment' of the Reformation; and each
generation must make sure that what is 'added' to the Gospel
in the process of interpretation does not in effect deprive it of
its savour.

Therefore the *Concessions to Melanchthon* are of crucial importance in Lutheranism. His person marks the turning point
in the history of the Reformation; having joined Luther in the
initial offensive where all things were counted loss in order to
win Christ, he proceeds to fortify the newly gained position by
using the material which the enemy left behind; he tries literally
to re-late the doctrine of the saving grace to tradition and reason,
to law and power. All the time he is watched in his systematic

efforts by the powerful party of the so-called Gnesiolutherans who accuse him of betraying the 'sola fide' of his master; and, indeed, at two points they have secured the official condemnation of the 'Philippists' by the Lutheran Church: in the synergist conception of free will and in the 'crypto-calvinist' conception of the eucharist. (So we shall have to disappoint the Anglican reader by leaving out of the picture two 'concessions' which are particularly dear to him on account of his inherent Pelagianism and of the Black Rubric in the Prayer Book.) But on the other side Melanchthon enjoys the unqualified confidence of Luther. He is the only humanist with whom he came to terms; and it must be said that in this strange alliance Melanchthon has proved the stronger influence in shaping the history of Lutheranism. Whether this was a blessing or a curse remains to be seen; we shall be wise not to blind ourselves by either of the traditional prejudices; he is neither a true copy nor a mere caricature of Luther. To see the difference will help us to correct the manifold superstitious views about the men of Wittenberg; to see the common ground enables us to define how far a Lutheran can go in humanism without becoming a heretic. The former is a lesson and a challenge, the latter an answer and a tribute to English critics of Lutheranism.

We must begin then by stating—not solving—the intricate problem of the friendship between Luther and Melanchthon. The prelude will be followed by the examination of the five main 'concessions' made by Melanchthon to elements outside the 'inner circle' of the evangelical faith; each of these headings reflects in some measure one of the inter-Lutheran controversies of the sixteenth century and still provides the key to central issues in Lutheran dogmatics. The last of the five chapters, 'Concessions to Opposition', points to an ultimate question which lies beyond the scope of this book: it is the part played by language in theology and in the separation or reunion of churches; the limit as to how far the 'being of one mind' is affected by speaking different tongues; in short, the question of the Church exclusive and comprehensive.

The theme is entirely doctrinal and not historical. Indeed, the historian will be grieved to find Melanchthon treated in precisely the same way as the Bible is treated by the bad preachers: the 'motto' is given out and then the text is left alone in order to plunge into 'problems'. My apology is that Melanchthon is not the Holy Scripture; he is not even Luther, whom to expound is always a treat; he is so intolerably dull in his endless rhetorical repetitions that quotations from his works must be severely rationed if the modern reader is to keep awake. He is not an original but a 'case'; attractive only because of the many problems with which he presented the Lutheran Church; therefore deserving to be dealt with both as subject and as object of our inquiry. The concessions made *to* Melanchthon are really made *by* him to the powers which he represents and which are far more important than he; what matters to decide is whether or not the Church is justified and bound to make these concessions to-day, rather than to describe in detail how, where and when Melanchthon was consistent and successful in making them.[1] So he figures deliberately as a dative in this book; it is written around him and not about him. As Lord Wedgwood said in the House of Lords on 21 May 1942: 'It is very beautiful when you find Marcus Aurelius providing you with a perfect quotation, but it is much more useful that you should discover that quotation for yourself, discover some of the truth for yourself.' And Melanchthon surely will not mind being found in this company.

[1] 'The Historical Point of View, put briefly, means that when a learned man is presented with any statement in an ancient author, the one question he never asks is whether it is true. He asks who influenced the ancient writer, and how far the statement is consistent with what he said in other books, and what phase in the writer's development, or in the general history of thought, it illustrates, and how it affected later writers, and how often it has been misunderstood (particularly by the learned man's own colleagues) and what the general course on it has been for the last ten years, and what is "the present state of the question"' (C. S. Lewis, *The Screwtape Letters*, pp. 139 sq.).

PRELUDE

THE FRIENDSHIP BETWEEN LUTHER AND MELANCHTHON

The puzzle is not so much the mutual attraction of two very different tempers, but the entry by, and reception of, Melanchthon into the headquarters of the Reformation; we are not concerned with the dramatic narrative of 'how they got on with each other' during the thirty years of their common residence in Wittenberg, but with the riddle of how their doctrines could 'mix'; with the astonishing fact that ever since they figure as joint partners of the firm 'Luther and Melanchthon' in such a way as none other of Luther's many colleagues could claim to be associated with him (the only conceivable comparison would be 'Luther and Calvin'). It remains to be seen whether the question which is obviously of modern origin will ever be properly answered; all we can try here is to find out how far it was felt to be a problem at the time of the Reformation, and to search what little material we have for hints in that direction.

We have the statement of a faithful Melanchthonian, Paul Eber, maintaining against the critics who 'equate Luther with gold, and much prefer this to Melanchthon's silver...; we know that Philippus, together with, and after Luther has produced optima fide integrum corpus doctrinae, bona et perspicua methodo et studio' (*CR*, 9, 966). On the other hand, there is a man like the Chancellor Brück denouncing in a letter to the elector prince of Saxony the heresies which Melanchthon himself had concealed from Luther: 'Doctor Martinus says and confesses, he had never thought that Philippus was still so deeply involved in the "phantasies"...I think there is no harm in Martinus still pressing on and giving a serious hearty talk to Philippus' (*CR*, 3, 427). The prince himself, no wonder, is so seriously worried by the reports of the 'Zweyung' between Luther and Melanchthon [1] that he goes so far as to contemplate the closing of

---

[1] 'If discord should grow between Lutherus and Philippus, God help us! What would come of it, how would the Papists glory and say: a kingdom divided against itself must perish. Also, no doubt, many Christian folk would take offence and stumble, even fall altogether away from the Gospel' (*CR*, 5, 502).

Wittenberg University, which would appear the lesser evil as compared with an open split in the faculty (*CR*, 3, 365 sqq.); at the same time he exerts the utmost pressure to prevent Luther from directly mentioning Melanchthon in his forthcoming pamphlet against the 'sacramentarians': 'Therefore it is our desire, and we want him to take our well-meant advice, that he should refrain from mentioning Philippus by name in his book...it is easy to see how the adversaries would rejoice over that and into what bad report the word of God would be brought' (*CR*, 5, 746 sq.). These three voices represent the views taken by the three parties in the Church struggles after Luther's death (the 'Philippists', the 'Gnesiolutherans' and the mediating statesmen) and echoed in all the subsequent literature on our subject.[1]

But what is the opinion of Luther and Melanchthon themselves? Consulting Luther's table-talks first, we find overwhelming evidence for the personal affection in which Melanchthon is held; the famous story that Luther prayed him back from death in a grave illness (*WA Ti*, 5, 5565, 5407) is of symbolic significance. So he won him over to Wittenberg in his youth and kept him by his spell; yet the impression which we are given

---

[1] It may be as well here to introduce the main figures of the inter-Lutheran controversies whose names, not often mentioned outside Germany, will frequently occur on the following pages. On Melanchthon's side we find Caspar Cruciger (Wittenberg; collaborator in Luther's translation of the Bible; his son succeeded Melanchthon as Professor); Paul Eber (Professor, General-superintendent and Hymn-writer in Wittenberg); Georg Major (Magdeburg, Wittenberg, Eisleben; his statement that good works are necessary to salvation caused the so-called Majorist dispute). The leaders of the 'Gnesiolutherans' are Nikolaus von Amsdorf, the first Lutheran Bishop (of Naumburg; who countered Major's statement by declaring good works to be harmful to salvation), and Matthias Flacius (Magdeburg and Jena; the first great Church historian of Lutheranism, author of the *Magdeburger Zenturionen*). Both oppose Melanchthon sharply in his attempts to compromise with Rome by accepting, in the so-called 'Interim' of Leipzig, a number of constitutional and ceremonial matters as non-essential ('Adiaphora'; 'adiaphorist' dispute). But they side with him against Andreas Osiander (Nürnberg and Königsberg, an uncle of Cranmer's wife) in defending 'imputed' against 'inherent' righteousness. Johann Brenz, the reformer of Württemberg, while opposing the 'Interim', tries to save Osiander from misinterpretation. Justus Jonas (Wittenberg, Halle, etc.; preached Luther's funeral sermon), the translator of Melanchthon's *Loci* and *Apologia*, belongs, in the 'Interim' controversy, to the opposite camp. Johann Agricola (Eisleben, Wittenberg and Berlin) is known for the three 'antinomian' disputations in which Luther defends Melanchthon against him and forces him to recant. Martin Bucer needs no introduction to Cambridge.

is as if Luther was entirely in Melanchthon's debt: we learn, for example, 'that D. Philippus had compelled him to translate the New Testament into German' (1, 961). The laudation of the great friend is not infrequently expressed in superlative terms: 'noster Philippus Melanchthon, homo admirabilis, imo paene nihil habens, quod non supra hominem sit... Philippus, quem non secus habeo ac me ipsum, excepta eruditione ac integritate vitae, qua me pudefacit, nedum superat' (*Letters*, ed. De Wette, I, 197; II, 407). It sounds as if Luther wanted us to picture himself as the barbarous peasant *vis-à-vis* the learned professor— which, incidentally, leads most people to make the wrong guess when comparing their two handwritings! His admiration for Melanchthon's writings is almost unqualified, whether it is the *Dialectica*,[1] the commentaries,[2] the *Confessio Augustana*[3] and the *Apologia*,[4] or, above all, the *Loci Communes* which Luther would like to translate himself (De Wette, II, 557) and which he does not hesitate to classify as the norm for all scripture reading.[5] 'Therefore who nowadays wants to be a theologian, has many advantages. First, he has the Bible made so plain that he can read it without any difficulty. Then he can read the *Loci Communes*; he should read them well and diligently so as to have them firmly in his head. If he has these two things, he is a theologian immune from the devil and all heretics, and the whole of theology lies open to him.... You find no book among all his books which comprises the sum of religion or the whole of theology as well as the *Loci*. All the Fathers and Commentators are just as nothing compared with that. Non est melior liber post scripturam sanctam quam ipsius loci communes' (*WA Ti*, 5, 5511; cf. 5647, 5787, 5827, 6439, 6458).

Luther's only word of regret is about Melanchthon's habit of dedicating his books to the potentates in State and Church, as e.g. to Henry VIII (the 1535 edition of the *Loci*, cf. *CR*, 2, 920) and Albrecht von Mainz (the 1532 commentary on Romans,

[1] 'Philippus fecit, quod nullus fecit in mille annis in dialectica.... Brevitatem et perspicuitatem I could not combine as well as Philippus.... Philippus superat omnes Graecos et Latinos in dialectica', *WA Ti*, 2, 1545, 1649, 2300.
[2] Particularly on Romans and Colossians: *WA Ti*, 1, 369; 4, 5007; 5, 5511.
[3] *WA Ti*, 2, 1481; De Wette, IV, 17.
[4] 'Apologia Philippi praestat omnibus doctoribus ecclesiae, etiam ipso Augustino', *WA Ti*, 1, 252.
[5] 'Ideo biblia sacra legenda iuxta locos communes Phil. Melanchthonis', *WA Ti*, 5, 6009; cf. 3, 3589, 3695.

cf. *CR*, 2, 611): 'I regret that Magister Philippus has dedicated
his best prefaces to the naughtiest boys' (*WA Ti*, 4, 4699). But
at the same time he defends him passionately from the charge
of corruptibility in connection with a royal donation received
from England: 'Et multa expendit in suos et alienos. Distribuit
eam pecuniam. Et dignus esset, cui regnum donaretur, tantus
vir et tam bene meritus de Romano imperio et ecclesia in tota
Germania et aliis regionibus!' (4, 4957). The friend in his eyes
is 'nimis modestus' (4, 4577; cf. 5, 5781): 'No one can repay his
labour. He must live in the alms house. Forsitan valeat ad pro-
movendum evangelium. Verecundus est. God help him! He
shall go to heaven, there he will be well rewarded; the world
shall not pay for his labour and work' (2, 1545). To the question
of a sceptic, 'si Philippus esset episcopus Saltzburgensis, an ita
liberalis maneret?', Luther replies firmly: 'Maxime! Nam habet
agnitionem Christi Jesu' (4, 4985).

Convinced of the essential soundness on the part of Melanchthon, Luther can afford to smile about some of his 'hobbies',
such as astrology: 'M. Ph. holds fast to it, but has never been
able to convince me' (1, 855). 'Neither Philippus nor anybody
else will ever persuade me to believe that it is a science....Illa
tota res est contra philosophiam' (5, 6250)—a statement no less
illuminating than the test of the two handwritings! The scholar
in Luther insists: 'Ego dixi: Foris nihil habent argumenti pro
astrologia nisi autoritatem Philippi. Tum Doctor: Ego saepe con-
futavi Philippum ita evidenter, ut diceret: Haec quidem vis est!
Et concessit esse scientiam, sed quam ipsi non teneant. Quare
ego sum contentus, si non tenent eam artem, so I allow him to
play with it...their art is all rubbish' (4, 5013). The believer is
even more outspoken: 'Ego puto, quod Philippus astrologica
tractat, sicut ego bibo *ein starcken trunck birs*, quando habeo
graves cogitationes' (1, 17). But the choice of the tonic by the
two men is not irrelevant. Of course what is true of astrology
is equally true of dreams: 'Luther praised that dream of Philippus
and said he had the gift of dreams, but I, he added, do not attribute
any weight to it. I do not care to have dreams and visions.
Certiora habeo, verbum Dei' (4, 4444b; cf. 5, 5494). Should this
be the root of the problem, that the 'solum verbum' was not
certain enough for Melanchthon?

But Luther continues to speak about a mere diversity of gifts
('varia dona', 1, 80), and to describe the difference in terms of

biblical analogies. 'Ego credo Paulum fuisse personam con-
temptibilem, a poor, thin, little man such as Philippus' (2, 1245)
must have sounded very flattering to Melanchthon, but fails to
impress us. Another comparison is surely nearer the mark:
'I am Isaiah, Philippus is Jeremiah; he always worried that he
scolded too much, just like Philippus!' (1, 887)—though again
the similarity between Philippus and Jeremiah can hardly be
pressed beyond this one point! More obvious is the parallel
drawn from Acts xv: 'Then they talked about the very different
minds of Luther and Melanchthon who had yet achieved the
maximum of concord. Luther replied: in the Acts of the Apostles
you have this picture: James denotes Philippus who with his
modesty would gladly have retained the law; Peter signifies
myself who brought it to fall. Why do you worry? Philippus
proceeds in charity, and I in faith. Philippus suffers himself to
be eaten up, I eat up everything and spare nobody. Et ita Deus
in diversis operatur idem' (4, 4577). Here we touch upon a
fundamental issue to which we shall have to come back: 'Multi
valde sudant, ut concordent Jacobum cum Paulo, velut etiam
Philippus in Apologia, sed non serio. Pugnantia sunt: fides
iustificat—fides non iustificat. Whoever can rhyme these two,
him will I decorate with my doctor's cap and let him call me a
fool' (3, 3292). Again, the different doctrinal emphasis—to put
it cautiously—corresponds to the divergence in the fields of
action: 'Diversum facit Philippus. Is meis negotiis non movetur,
sed movent eum illa grandia reipublicae et religionis. Me privata
tantum premunt. Sic sunt varia dona' (1, 80).[1]

Thus a peculiar *modus agendi* is necessitated on which Luther
makes some further observations. It occurs only once that he
has to blame Melanchthon for too much rigidity, and that is,
significantly enough, in his capacity as examiner.[2] In all other
respects 'de Philippo omnium judicium hoc est: si peccat, tunc
lenitate peccat. He is too easily taken in. His little scholarly
instruments are not good enough; the trunks demand an axe'
(5, 6443). As it fell upon Melanchthon to represent the Protestant cause in nearly all official negotiations, this became of

[1] Cf. 3, 3809: 'L. negabat se esse administratorem.'
[2] 'Therefore I am pleased when the young people and students produce
arguments, however good or bad they might be, and I dislike Philippus
examining so strictly and sharply as to rush over the poor fellows;
one must climb stairs step by step, nobody can be at once on top',
4, 4056.

crucial importance. Luther's criticism of the *Augustana*, 'I cannot tread so softly' (De Wette, IV, 17) is well known. It had to be repeated on more than one occasion. When he tarried at the Hagenau convent in 1540, Luther remarked: 'Philippus vult mori in hac synodo et fecit versum. Sed nostrum Paternoster erit fortius cogitationibus Philippi' (4, 5058; cf. 5062, 5096, 5091, 5054). Eventually Melanchthon seemed to be converted to Luther's methods: 'Ph. has finally fallen foul of the Papists. For a while he wanted to deal with the case according to his equity; now he sees that nothing will help with these scoundrels' (4, 4909). But Luther's reflection is based upon something more than the practical success when he turns to Melanchthon's manner of polemics: 'Philippus, too, pricks, but with needles only; the pricks hurt and are hard to heal; but I stab with boars' spears' (1, 348). Long after Luther's death experience confirmed his suspicion 'that Philippus too much indulges in affections and bears the cross more impatiently than becomes a disciple, or rather, such a master of so many' (De Wette, II, 29; see below, pp. 66, 79).

Leaving aside these wider moral and political implications, we must try to understand what it means that Luther and Melanchthon talk in two different languages. The fact at least was realized by both. 'In tractatione scripturae ego vehementior sum quam Philippus, etsi in libello de ecclesia (1539) acrior fuit. Sententia eius libri est vehemens, sed verba videntur mihi non esse similia rebus; sed non intelligo vim Latini sermonis' (*WA Ti*, 4, 5054). But we are faced not with the simple question of the 'vis Latini sermonis',[1] but with the fundamental problem whether in reality 'verba videntur non esse similia rebus'. Is it only the language which separates Melanchthon from Luther or does he say something altogether different? Luther's summary reply seems to leave no doubt and is striking both in matter and in form: 'Res et verba Philippus; verba sine re Erasmus; res sine verbis Lutherus; nec res nec verba Carolostadius' (3, 3619). And the final verdict runs: 'Ego hoc didici experientia: *Quotquot M. Philippo et mihi adversati* sunt e nostris, exciderunt a fide' (4, 4946; cf. 5, 5788). The solidarity with Melanchthon is so firmly established that his dissent from Amsdorf and Agricola can be dismissed in the uncommonly irenic phrase: 'I do not think

---

[1] In another passage Luther makes the distinction: 'Tu rhetor es scribendo, non dicendo...sed quae scripseram, Philippo non placebant' (2, 2068).

much of this strife of words, particularly among the people'
(De Wette, III, 215); that the Elector's clemency is pleaded for
Philippus in a moment of grave mismanagement;[1] that even in
the sacramental dispute the other side is rebuked for its imperti-
nent claim 'se cum Philippo et Luthero sentire' (*WA Ti*, 3, 3231),
as if there were but one mind and one mouth to consider. However inconspicuous and inconsistent may have been the part which
the virtue of tolerance played in Luther's life, in the case of
Melanchthon he acted literally and thoroughly according to his
words: 'Ego soleo dissimulare et celare, quantum possum, ubi
aliqui nostrum vere dissentiunt a nobis' (De Wette, II, 522).[2]
The only possible explanation for that course must be sought in
an amazing capacity to read his own 'res' into and behind
Melanchthon's 'verba'. Was his trust justified? Was he right
in his optimism: 'What do we lack, Philippus, I, Doctor Jonas,
Major? Are we not getting on well?' (*WA Ti*, 5, 5476).[3] Or
had he any sinister forebodings when he once asked: 'How is
it that he is the worst deceiver whom one had trusted most?'
and when Melanchthon answered: 'Optime scribit Xenophon:
facis id, quod est facillimum, amico iniuriam...' (4, 3938). In
another, more harmless and objective, table-talk the tragedy of
the second generation is well described: 'But Phil. said to Luther:
My dear Doctor, there are godly people who die in the knowledge of Christ, and particularly young people; for the older we
become, the more foolish we are. The young folk stick simply
to the articles of the Christian faith; as they have learnt them, so
they believe them; but when we grow old, we begin to dispute,
want to be clever, while we are the greatest fools' (5, 5563).
That is the Reformation itself in the process of 'growing old'—
and so we come to look at our problem with the eyes of Melanchthon.

The picture, for all its parallels, is different from the outset.
Here, too, we have the symbolic incident of Melanchthon watching
a serious illness of Luther, yet, notwithstanding Luther's emphatic tribute, 'Ph. me uno verbo erigit' (*CR*, 1, 360), he is not
powerful enough to pray him back from death, but, 'when he

[1] 'For they have maintained our dear Confession and did abide firmly
by it, even if everything else went wrong' (De Wette, V, 357).
[2] Melanchthon, on the other hand, had his moments when he could say:
'non soleo dissimulare, quid de controversia illa sentiam' (*CR*, 1, 946)!
[3] Cf. Luther's remarks on the future of the Wittenberg faculty, ibid.
5, 5423; 4, 5126.

looked at him dissolved into tears' (*WA Ti*, 3, 3543). There is
a sigh of relief in his exclamation: 'so far, thank God, Martinus
breathes, so pray that he may go on breathing, ille unicus θεολόγου
διδασκαλίας vindex' (*CR*, 1, 208)—and the corresponding sigh
of despair after Luther's death when a new and trying era of the
Church is dawning (cf. 11, 783 ff.: 'De Luthero et aetatibus
ecclesiae'). 'I would die rather than be separated from this man;
nothing more trist could happen than to have to do without
Martinus' (1, 160, 269) is the refrain of many testimonies which
show a genuine sense of dependence upon 'hoc Hercule nostro'
(1, 282). It is noteworthy that of all comparisons this comes first
to Melanchthon's mind; he can never escape the impression of
overpowering physical and spiritual strength. 'Martinus seems
to me to be driven by a spirit...impossible for me not to fall in
love with him' (1, 269, 96); but these almost naïve understate-
ments soon give way to the flourish of his Latin rhetoric: 'ne
ille opprimatur, vir unus, quem ego ausim et vere non modo
omnibus huius aetatis, sed omnibus omnium seculorum, omnium
temporum vel Augustinis, vel Hieronymis, vel Nazianzenis prae-
ferre' (1, 270). Solon, Themistocles, Scipio and Augustus, however great their empires, are far inferior to 'nostris ducibus Jesaia,
Baptista, Paulo, Augustino, Luthero' (11, 728). And the praise
of the man is the praise of his doctrine. 'For when we study
Luther, we deal with the cause of true theology and Christian
doctrine, which he, in the spirit of Elijah, has plainly asserted;
I have never had any doubt whatsoever about Luther's integrity
or the truth of his doctrine' (1, 287, 598); yes, even 'you grieve
the Holy Spirit, not Luther, when you take offence at this'
(1, 320; cf. 1002). All this appears to be strictly in line with
the later orthodoxy of Wittenberg: 'God's Word and Luther's
doctrine shall never pass away',[1] and with the tendency which
leads certain dogmatics to the conception of a 'Locus de Vocatione Lutheri'.

Yet Melanchthon gives himself away when in the course of his
necrologies on Luther he makes the confession: 'Cumque deces-
serit Lutherus ἐν εὐφημίᾳ bonos et amantes Deum etiam de viro
tanto, qui certe aliquam doctrinae celestis partem illustravit, decet

---

[1] 'Gottes Wort und Luthers Lehr vergehen nun und nimmermehr.' On
the origin of the famous formula see O. Ritschl, *Dogmengeschichte des
Protestantismus*, II, 356, note 3; and R. Seeberg, *Dogmengeschichte*, IV,
part II, p. 435.

εὔφημα dicere' (*CR*, 6, 80). Thus the adherence to the master is qualified in two important ways. First, 'decet εὔφημα dicere'—in marked contrast to Luther's own deplorable manner of speaking. 'Nunquam ita amavi Lutherum, ut veluti instruxerim eius in disputatione vehementiam' (1, 946). The disputations and pamphlets themselves become a nightmare to him; more than once he unburdens his heart in letters to Camerarius, his 'intimus': 'you are quite right in guessing that these harsh addresses (sc. Lutheri dissidia cum Iurisconsultis de clandestinis sponsalibus) are a cause of great grievance to me. Many things trouble me. What is the use of it all to the people? How very inopportune is the moment, when big decisions seem to be pending' (5, 310 sq.). We seem to hear the gentle voice of a British critic when we read: 'this cause could be pleaded in a more civil way' (1, 1023). While defending Luther's superiority against a popular overestimate of Erasmus,[1] he cannot help holding, like the latter, Luther's polemics responsible for the drive of many people into the opposite camp:[2] and both in the sacramental issue and in the conflict 'de libero arbitrio' Melanchthon himself must vote for appeasement.[3] 'How this conflicts with your statement, I cannot see even now' (3, 68 sq.) is one of his typical sentences written to Erasmus, with whom he maintained an unbroken correspondence.

The second qualification is that Luther 'certe *aliquam* doctrinae celestis *partem* illustravit', and again Melanchthon's friendship with Erasmus is a striking reminder of that. 'I have, during and after Luther's lifetime, rejected the Stoic and Manichean "deliria", presented by Luther and others, that all works, good and evil, in all men, good and evil, had to come about by necessity. It is obvious that such phrases are against the word of God, harmful to all discipline, and blasphemous' (9, 766; similarly 8, 916). This criticism deserves attention, not so much because of its particular theme but because of its general principle. 'God's Word' and 'Luther's doctrine' are not simply identical; the latter

---

[1] 'Quae fortasse longe graviores tumultus aliquando excitatura fuerant, nisi Lutherus exortus esset.'

[2] 'Tota illa tragoedia περὶ δείπνου κυριακοῦ ab ipso nata videri potest' (1, 1083); Erasmus's words.

[3] Melanchthon to Erasmus: 'De scriptis contra te hic editis quod fuerit meum iudicium, eo nihil hic dico, quia non solum propter privata officia, sed etiam propterea displicuerunt, quia tanta scripta sunt inutilia reipublicae. Neque hoc iudicium meum dissimulavi unquam' (3, 69).

is judged by the former. Now the laudations of Luther, without
losing their weight and sincerity, must be viewed in a different
light: 'I should not want you to favour Luther unless it is because
you feel bound to favour the truth of the Gospel... while Mon-
tanus wanted people to believe him, Luther wanted not himself,
but scripture in its evidence and perspicuity to be believed'
(1, 287, 406); 'volebat enim Lutherus non detinere (nos) in suis
scriptis, sed ad fontes deducere omnium mentes; ipsam vocem
Dei audire nos voluit' (6, 170). Of course this is precisely what
Luther himself had said and how he wanted to be understood;
and it is also the criterion of Lutheranism as a whole, established
in the preface to the *Formula Concordiae*.[1] But it is significant
that Melanchthon should be the first to apply the criterion in
terms of a censure on parts of Luther's own writings.

He did not do it with an easy mind. 'Non sum natura φιλόνεικος;
I am a quiet bird' (6, 880; 5, 474). But Luther, he thought, fell
under that ominous category of the φιλόνεικος, and he, Melanchthon, felt very much his victim. 'I have also borne the
almost shameful servitude, since Luther often served his nature
(in which there was no small φιλονεικία) rather than what was
good for his own person or the community' (6, 880) is an out-
burst two years after Luther's death which no biographer of
Melanchthon could fail to register. It was, however, not different
while Luther was alive. 'Πολλάκις σημαίνει τὴν παλαιὰν ὀργήν'
(3, 595); 'omissis igitur ἃ μετεχειρίζοντο nunc βροντᾶται καὶ
ἀστράπτεται καθ' ἑτέρων τινῶν, interdum me quoque petendo'
(5, 462). And Cruciger confirms his suspicions: 'Luther calls
the mediators Erasmians, no doubt aiming at us, and most
of all at Philippus' (3, 397). But worst of all was the agitation
of the anti-Philippist party which began early and grew in-
tolerable in his last lonely years. 'Amsdorf has written to Luther
to say that he was nursing a snake in his bosom, denoting myself:
I leave out the rest' (3, 503). The charges were both moral and
doctrinal. 'Some suspect me of taking favours from the mighty
...and to have been corrupted with money by Iulius, the Bishop
of Naumburg' (5, 332; 7, 352); against which we remember
Luther's fervent defence of Melanchthon (see above, p. xviii).
More heavily than these 'falsissimae calumniae certorum sycophan-

---

[1] Cf. *Symbolische Bücher der Evangelisch-Lutherischen Kirche*, ed. J. T.
Müller, and the corresponding preamble of the Barmen Declaration of the
Confessional Church.

tarum' weighs the charge against the *Augsburg Confession* and
Apologia: 'Dicor nimium laudare bona opera' (5, 754). The reply
is: 'Utinam satis laudarem!' Although Melanchthon stoically
quotes the story of Flavianus Antiochenus, who, accused before
Theodosius, declared that he would suffer reproof of his doctrine
or morals, but give up the fight when 'de dignitate καὶ περὶ
προεδρίας est certamen' (3, 459), the atmosphere of Wittenberg
made it hard enough for him to remain calm. 'Noster Cyzizensis,'
writes Cruciger about Amsdorf, 'ut est rigidus, etiam τὸν ἡμέτερον
διδάσκαλον (Lutherum) inflammavit....Itaque constituit alter
(Melanchthon), se potius recta pedibus egressurum esse urbem,
quam sic assentiatur aut pugnet cum διδασκάλῳ' (5, 477; cf. 484).
The question of emigration arose more than once: 'Which of us
has a safe abode? For about fifteen years I have daily expected
expulsion, and am still expecting it' (6, 860).

As the date of the fifteen years indicates, the position was all
the more difficult since Luther was no longer there; in fact, it
was ultimately the bond with him which held Melanchthon in
Wittenberg.[1] This implied not only mutual loyalty and support
in the sphere of personal relations, but an emphatic claim by
Melanchthon to be the true and genuine representative of the
Lutheran tradition: 'I have always maintained the contents of
the *Commentarius Inspectionis Ecclesiarum* to be in complete
accordance with Luther's doctrine...si quis Lutherum recantare
aliquid in meo opere iudicat, is multipliciter insanit. Si quid
scriptum est, quod videtur pugnare cum Lutheri doctrina, id ad
me, non ad Lutherum pertinet' (1, 898). The real divergences are
about some Adiaphora;[2] here Melanchthon feels free to make his
own comments on 'aliquam doctrinae celestis partem', and
here Luther seems to have agreed to disagree. 'Neither does
Luther seem to bear us any hostility. Yesterday he spoke very
amiably about these controversies with me...when I pointed
out what a tragic spectacle it would be to see us fight with one
another like the Cadmean brothers. You know that I speak less
harshly about predestination, free will, necessity of obedience,
and original sin. In all these matters as such, Luther, I know,

[1] Cf. F. Galle, *Melanchthon, Versuch einer Charakteristik Melanchthons
als Theologen*, Halle, 1845, p. 146, n. 2.

[2] See above, p. xvi. 'De Adiaphoris ideo minus contendimus, quia alia
maiora certamina sustinemus.... Obsecro te, concordiam inter vos tueamur,
nec propter Adiaphora inter nos ipsi dimicemus', letter to Hardenberg, *CR*,
7, 357; cf. ibid. 9, 763 sq.: 'Bedenken auf das Weimarer Confutationsbuch.'

thinks as I do, but the uneducated too much prefer some of his
more vehement phrases, the point of which they do not understand. I do not think it is for me to fight them; they may use
their own judgment. Mihi tamen concedant homini Peripatetico,
et amanti mediocritatem, minus Stoice alicubi loqui. That is the
sum of the matter' (*CR*, 3, 383). It is indeed the 'summa negotii'
because it shows clearly that Melanchthon's 'contribution' to
Lutheranism is both to complete and to polish what Luther said;
the key lies in the references to the 'homo peripateticus' and to
the 'modus dicendi': 'scis me quaedam minus horride dicere';
thus the defects of Luther's φιλονεικία are overcome. The next
passage makes the same vital point in still more positive terms:
'When we in our first visitation of the churches found so many
conflicting voices among the uneducated about many points, I
drew up a summa doctrinae in one volume which Luther had
delivered in various volumes of commentaries and addresses; et
quaesivi genus verborum, quo ad proprietatem, quae ad perspicuitatem et concordiam utilis est, discentes assuefierent, ac
semper omnia scripta iudicio Ecclesiae nostrae et ipsius Lutheri
permisi: de multis quaestionibus etiam diserte sciscitatus sum
Lutherum, quid sentiret, ac multi pagellarum illarum exempla
adhuc habent' (7, 479). In other words, Melanchthon describes
his work as the quest for a new 'genus verborum' which is apt
to summarize and harmonize the doctrines of the Reformation;
his task, in succession to Luther, is to restate the case in the proper
language.

In a letter from which we quoted on the previous page, he uses
the very distinction between 'res et verba' and 'res sine verbis'
which we have heard from Luther.[1] 'Lenitas' was, as we have
seen, Luther's only charge against him. So we are again left with
the question whether or not they both said the same thing in
different words. 'Rem ipsam semper retinui' (7, 756 sq.) was
Melanchthon's defence in an argument about the 'sola fide'. But
that he is on the defence all the time appears to be the decisive
factor in his relation to Luther. It lends colour to all his utterances,

---

[1] See above, p. xx. 'Tantum me hoc cavisse, ut sine acerbitate verborum,
res nudae proponerentur. Multae mihi causae fuerunt eius lenitatis...mihi
magis fuit spectandum, quid Deo placeret, quam quando sycophantas illos
mihi placarem, a quibus nunc ut hereticus, ut fanaticus traducor. Hanc meam
epistolam potes exhibere quibus velis....Et Lutherus mihi optimus testis
est, me semper optasse in hac tota dissensione, ut summa lenitate nostri
omnes uterentur' (*CR*, 1, 898).

and it places them in marked contrast to the corresponding words
of Luther about Melanchthon. A scene reported in the table-
talks may serve as illustration. 'D. Caspar (Cruciger) said to
Philippus that he could hardly bear his presence in his lectures.
Then said Luther: Neither am I very keen to have him in my
lectures, but I cross myself and think: Philippus, Jonas, Pommer [1]
are not in here, and I imagine that no wiser man stands on the
cathedra than myself' (*WA Ti*, 3, 2954 b). Luther is so sure of
his teaching that he can safely ignore the presence of his learned
colleague, and again, he is so sure of Melanchthon that he can
safely leave it to him what he makes of the lecture: 'Philippus
non est docendus, nec ego propter illum doceo aut lego' (*WA Ti*,
4, 5047). Melanchthon's position is just the reverse. One could
not imagine that he would have happily lectured in front of
Luther. He would have felt that he had to prove his orthodoxy—
as he repeatedly admits: 'semper omnia scripta iudicio Ecclesiae
nostrae et ipsius Lutheri permisi'—and should Luther have taken
notes, Melanchthon would most surely have corrected them.
Certainty on his side is lacking in the same measure in which
it abounds with Luther; he tests where Luther trusts; he takes
control of the depositum fidei which Luther generously leaves to
him, and so he comes to determine the future of Lutheranism.
The change of language is therefore of the most far-reaching
psychological and theological importance; and it is from this
direction that the puzzle 'Luther and Melanchthon' which we
leave now will have to be approached for its solution.

[1] 'Doctor Pommer' (Pomeranus), nickname for Bugenhagen, the chief
Pastor of Wittenberg and Reformer of Denmark, in whose frequent absence
Luther deputized in the pulpit of the Stadtkirche at Wittenberg.

CHAPTER I

CONCESSIONS TO TRADITION

A. THE SCHOOL OF GREECE

Among the powers which Melanchthon undertakes to reconcile with Luther's 'sola fide', tradition holds obviously the first place. It confronts the Reformation from two sides: from the humanist movement and from the official Church. Both influences have worked together to shape Melanchthon's past, and they represent the twofold inheritance of our civilization which he wanted to preserve and to transmit: the school of Greece and the school of Rome.

Of course we must not judge him from his earliest pronouncements. To enter Wittenberg means for the young Professor (he is just over twenty!) to say good-bye to 'classics'.[1] He takes great pleasure in editing Aristophanes' *Clouds* and declares in his preface: 'What is the use to the nation of those disputations about ideas, space, clouds and other such useless theories? Nam philosophiam, si propius contempleris, videas nihil esse nisi stultas frivolarum opinionum pugnas. Should we to whom is given from heaven a peculiar faculty of discernment cherish that godless and useless thing as if it were the pattern of the divine mind?' (*CR*, 1, 273 sq.). But this mood does not last very long. His own words, in the closing sentence of our quotation, suggest that he is bound to follow his master St Paul from the insistence 'that your faith should not stand in the wisdom of men' (1 Cor. ii, 5) to the very next verse: 'Howbeit we speak wisdom among them that are perfect.' The step had to be taken quite practically because Melanchthon's lecturing duties inevitably reopened the contact with the Greeks. And as early as 1523, when Luther tries to claim him exclusively for theology, we find him replying: 'Tamen optarim a praelectionibus theologicis liberari. Primum enim agnosco, quam sim maximis rebus tractandi impar, planeque ipse mihi videor κατὰ παροιμίαν asinus esse, qui Mysteria gerat.

[1] 'Id ut conveniat cum Aristotelis philosophia, non laboro. Quid enim ad me quid senserit ille rixator?' (*CR*, 21, 117). '...qui e Theologica nobis non aliud fecere, quam illam Graeciae hircissantem anum, Philosophiam' (11, 38).

Deinde tanta turba est praelectorum theologicorum, ut obruatur potius quam doceatur iuventus. Postremo aptior fortasse fuerim ad docendas pueriles literas. Habes quid censeam' (1, 607; cf. 575, 677). One would suspect the desire to escape the *rabies theologorum* to have been a strong additional reason. The argument of professional circles is anticipated: 'But how can you, homo theologus, take up philosophy? Don't you know that there is a war, and what a war, between philosophy and the theologians at this time?... To be honest, I take great delight in those ancient scripts, and often deplore the stupidity of an age which allowed such glorious monuments to be obliterated. I often look at my books which surely are no less dear to me than my children (!) and reflect, what the second-hand booksellers might not perhaps make of them' (1, 695). There is already evidence of a barbarous and sophisticated age in theology,[1] the description of which is by no means out of date: 'Bone Deus! quam prepostera theologicantur, qui solo rerum bonarum contemptu sapere videri volunt!' (1, 613). Of that danger the academic youth must be warned and made to see the incomparable educational value of ancient philosophy: 'The worst of all evils is an uneducated theology[2]... such a doctrine cannot help producing infinite errors...my judgment is that the tender minds must be imbued with the doctrine of Aristotle, the value of which will outdo all the other sects' (11, 280; 3, 362). The time has come to rediscover the true Aristotle purified from the 'many absurd opinions' of the scholastic commentators (9, 700), and to present him to students as the pattern of real philosophy: 'Nobis autem consilium videtur e media Graecia deligere optimae notae classicos, qui et ad linguae cultum, et ad vitae rationes formandas pertinent' (1, 74; cf. 53).

It may well be questioned how far Melanchthon succeeded in this task and whether the Aristotelianism of the Lutheran orthodoxy was so very much more worthy of its name than that of the scholastic commentaries; Melanchthon's own picture of his

---

[1] 'Ac plane dignos esse odio censeo Anabaptistas, et si qui similes sunt, qui ineruditam et barbaricam theologiam in Ecclesiam invehere conantur, et contendunt nullis literis opus esse. Quare omnia confuse sine arte dicunt, nullam adhibent antiquitatis notitiam, nullam collationem ex aliis disciplinis' (2, 926). This anarchism in education corresponds, of course, exactly to that in politics, and Melanchthon, as we shall see in Chapter IV A, is equally averse to both.

[2] Compare, for a modern parallel, the prominence of this sentiment in H. Hensley Henson's *Retrospect of an Unimportant Life*.

hero is anything but genuine and original.[1] But this is not our problem. The important aspect is the reaction to the Greeks of which Melanchthon is typical, the dialectic tension between Wittenberg and Athens of which his case is but the first example in the history of Protestantism. Luther had spoken and maintained his solemn anathema against 'that heathen Aristotle' (*WA Ti*, 5, 6479, 6481), and yet it is with his full knowledge that Melanchthon bases the whole training of the following generations on the axiom: 'carere igitur Aristotelis monumentis non possumus' (*CR*, 11, 654). In a wider respect the aim of the Reformation can be interpreted as the final break of the medieval synthesis between Christianity and Hellenism; and, on the other hand, an authoritative humanist scholar to-day ascribes to Huguenot France and Protestant Germany 'the break through to Hellenism'.[2] Indeed, the cry 'ad fontes' indicates a parallel move in the Reformation and in Humanism; we remember Melanchthon's use of the term in his description of Luther's work (see above, p. xxiv). And the parallel is more than formal: how could Luther's work have ever been done without Reuchlin's Hebrew Grammar and Erasmus' Greek New Testament? Had not Luther said himself: 'as dear as the Gospel is to us, so hard let us hold to the languages'? (*WA*, xv, 37, 17 sq.). Moreover, Greek was in a fundamental sense the language in which the central dogma of the Church had found its expression, and far from abandoning the dogma, the reformers preserved all the traditional formulae, sometimes, as in Luther's Christology and eucharistic doctrine, developing them with a distinct tendency towards specific Greek trends of thought.

Here, however, lies what many critics have regarded as the fatal deficiency of the reformers, and here begin the attempts 'to finish the Reformation'. It is the Greek dress which is supposed to be inadequate to the essence of the Gospel, and the demand is for a new genuine terminology to fit the dogma of the Christian Church. In this view Kant appears to be the great philosopher of Protestantism; from him, not from Luther, dates the beginning of the modern age; he is the decisive factor in the *Ueberwindung*

[1] 'Et hanc fuisse Aristoteli causam arbitror, cur methodum adeo exiliter consectaretur, ut ea quae a Platone acceperat, collecta, et quadam oeconomia atque ordine distributa, posteris integre traderet. Etsi quaedam limare etiam ac corrigere voluit, rerum tantum in summa non magna est dissimilitudo. Non difficile est prudentibus videre, uter in qua parte praestet' (*CR*, 11, 423).

[2] Werner Jaeger, *Humanistische Reden und Vorträge*, 1937, pp. 25, 182.

der Antike. His discovery, so often compared to that of Copernicus, marks the turn from substance to subject, from dogmatism to criticism, from cosmology to anthropology, from 'mysticism' to ethics. The whole system renders the Greek categories obsolete, and it seems difficult to overrate the change which this must mean when applied to such terms as 'person' and 'nature' in the dogmatic concepts of Trinity and Christology.[1] Even the most emphatic anti-modernists who otherwise have little use for Kant in theology hail his final disestablishment of metaphysics as a lasting benefit both to faith and reason; it was in ecclesiastical circles that the neo-Kantianism of the Marburg School came to enjoy its latest triumphs. What they failed to see was the complementary historical function of Kant, his eminently positive role as true heir to the Greek tradition as counterpart to Socrates in the fight against scepticism, and the consequent emergence of a new Platonism and Aristotelianism in the school of his successors—in short, the constructive significance of the 'critical philosophy' which prepared the way for the new metaphysics of Fichte, Schelling and Hegel. Held against the background of the degenerated philosophy of the last hundred years, it becomes evident why Kant and his followers still rank in the popular phrase with the 'classical' thinkers.

So the result, if not the aim, of the idealistic movement is a new synthesis between Christianity and Hellenism,[2] and once again the next generation makes it its task to break the alliance. The reaction, in theology, begins with Kierkegaard and has not even now reached its end. It has almost become a criterion of orthodoxy to purge one's vocabulary from any Greek elements; words like 'idea', 'system', 'principle', 'theory' are anxiously avoided. Current talk is in terms of historicity (*Geschichtlichkeit*)—which, alas, does not mean that the new theological language is either more lucid or more beautiful. There is, however, a connection between these more vulgar phenomena of our days and the standard work of Harnack which views the whole *Dogmengeschichte* as the process of 'acute Hellenization of Christianity'.[3] The obvious difference of opinion at present is about

[1] See, for example, Emanuel Hirsch, *Jesus Christus der Herr*, 1926, pp. 47 sqq.

[2] Cf. R. Kroner, *Von Kant zu Hegel*, 1924, II, 255 sq.

[3] Thus itself reviving early Lutheran concepts of Church history as the one great example of apostasy; cf. Gottfried Arnold's *Unparteiische Kirchen- und Ketzergeschichte*.

the contents and extent of the Greek elements rather than about
the method of their elimination from the Gospel; the 'purist'
tendency still prevails in spite of a totally new definition of the
'Wesen des Christentums'; and the question is not whether, but
where, the line must be drawn which separates the preaching of
Jesus from the wisdom of the Greeks. Harnack's idea of the two
Gospels within the New Testament has long been abandoned;
instead, the unity of the apostolic kerygma has been established,
and the whole New Testament is being interpreted on the strength
of its Jewish origin and environment in marked contrast to the
Greek world. Dogmatic interest is turning from patristics to
exegetics, and here again from Hellenistics to Rabbinics; all
parties and sects among the younger German theologians agree
in their unanimous praise of Schlatter, who has cleared the field
from what he called 'Greek thinking'; and in his school Gerhard
Kittel, for all his notorious anti-semitism, displays but the
German variety of Judaistic Christianity.

Indeed, this latest phase in Protestant theology manifests most
clearly the urgency of the problem, 'The Gospel and the Greeks',
and the inner logic of history will not allow the solution to be of
a one-sided negative kind; sooner or later we are bound to state
our relation to the school of Greece in positive terms. At this
point Melanchthon may have a valuable lesson to teach us. What
is it, we ask him, that gives in his eyes that paramount importance to Greek philosophy? Why could the Lutheran Church
throughout four centuries never entirely free itself from this part
of its tradition? Melanchthon has no hesitation in replying quite
directly in a reference to Galen: 'veterem Philosophiam, *hoc est
veritatem*, adversus eorum (sc. Stoic. et Epicur.) deliria propugnat'
(*CR*, 11, 653), and he adds, in another reference to Aristotle:
'Hanc igitur doctrinam, quae quasi vox est naturae, sequamur'
(13, 381). This defence of 'veritas' and 'vox naturae' implies, of
course, the repudiation of all ancient and modern sophistry:
'I require an educated philosophy, not those sophistications which
have nothing in them. Therefore I have said one must select one
definite kind of philosophy, which has the least use for sophistications and retains the right method: such is the doctrine of
Aristotle' (11, 282).[1] A threefold test is required in order to
distinguish true philosophy from idle speculation: demonstra-

[1] Cf. 3, 914: 'Me ludi illi, ac Sophistarum praestigiae non delectant, nec
tam cupio esse φίλιππος quam φιλαλήθης.'

bility,[1] moderation[2] and unity.[3] The last point is taken by Melanchthon in the literal sense that only one of the historical schools of wisdom can possibly be right, and that it is therefore the moral duty of the philosopher to commit himself to one master.[4] A thorough inquiry into the chief philosophical 'sects' (13, 655 sqq.) leads to the selection of Aristotle—a choice which is confirmed by the vote of history: 'vir animi sagax Aristoteles, ut hunc nominem, in quem opinio hominum consentiens multis iam seculis conspiravit' (11, 8).

The way to arrive at this conclusion is by comparison of the Stoics, Epicurus, the Academy and Aristotle under the three headings: dialectics, physics, ethics. Melanchthon, in his philosophical commentaries, follows that traditional division. His only criticisms of Aristotle are against the 'argumenta de aeternitate mundi' (13, 222 sq., 376 sq.) and against making the 'materia elementorum' the philosophical point of departure;[5] in both cases the biblical revelation demands and provides the correction.[6] But the divergence is not anything like as fundamental as it would seem to the eyes of modern science on the one side and to 'theocentric' insight on the other. Not only is Melanchthon utterly conservative in maintaining the Ptolemean world view against Copernicus,[7] but his love for astronomy drives him so far as to

---

[1] 'Itaque philosophiam vocamus non omnes omnium opiniones, sed tantum hanc doctrinam, quae habet demonstrationes', 12, 690.

[2] '...eligere sectam, quae studium habeat non rixandi, sed inquirendae veritatis, deinde quae amet moderatas opiniones', 11, 283.

[3] 'Verum autem unum est, ut dicunt philosophi, quare una tantum philosophia vera est', 12, 690.

[4] 'Sed clamant aliqui, ut apes ex magna varietate florum succos colligunt, ita doctrinam ex variis sectis excerpendam esse. Hi refutandi sunt hoc ipso exemplo, ut enim apes natura duce vitant venena, ita nos praelucente Deo, vitemus falsas opiniones. Quia autem, ut unumquenque decet civitatis certae ac bene moratae civem esse, ita decet certae et honestae scholae auditorem dici, Aristotelicos non(nos?) esse profiteamur et sectas diiudicemus', 13, 656.

[5] 'Aristoteles a materia exorsus est, et quaestiones de Deo, de Coelo, de Stellis differt in posteriores libros.... Sed nos a Deo ordiri maluimus, ut a prima causa, ad ceteros deinde progrederemur', 13, 197; cf. 195.

[6] (a) 'Adsentiamur autem doctrinae a Deo traditae, quae ait hunc mundum conditum esse etc. Haec sententia extra iudicium humanae rationis posita est' (13, 222). (b) 'Cumque in omnibus honestis rebus suscipiendis, auxilium Dei petendum sit, maxime in hac naturae consideratione, mentes nostrae a Deo aeterno patre, Domini nostri Jesu Christi, architecto universae naturae gubernari petemus' (13, 197, 198).

[7] 'Sumus autem secuti in describendis illis Ptolemaei hypotheses, quae tot seculorum testimonio comprobatae, non temere convelli debent', 13, 292 (cf. 276, 216, 244, 228).

speak of 'illa praestantissima Philosophiae pars, de motibus coelestibus' (11, 282). The 'physica Aristotelis', of which Luther had remarked that it was 'a totally useless matter for any age' (De Wette, 1, 239), is faithfully reproduced by Melanchthon; and Galen earns the compliment that he 'had most wisely declared the teaching of anatomy to be the beginning of theology and the gateway towards the knowledge of God' (CR, 11, 501). We, of course, find it very difficult to overlook the fact that the obvious limitations of the Greek school lie with its concept of 'physics', and that the true search for the 'initium' begins in quite a different chapter of their philosophy; it is in dialectics that they have made their essential contribution. 'Quaeso quid praestat ubique vel aptius vel eruditius Dialectica [sc. Aristotelis]?' (11, 8).[1] If the crude parable is permissible, we may imagine Kant looking to the Greeks with a sense of indebtedness similar to that of Mr Churchill towards America: 'give us the tools, and we will finish the job!' They have given us the 'tools' in the form of the categories without which the 'job' of thinking could not be carried out; and their merit is not only the method of abstraction and the perspicuity of expression,[2] but the consummation of all dialectics in the supreme idea of the Logos. Thus the key-word is produced which alone can bring order into the chaos; philosophy becomes inevitably systematic, and this, so far from being a merely 'formal' significance, is a means of preparation for the Gospel. Heraklitos—whatever Bultmann says—stands literally 'next door' to the prologue of St John. We shall have to define later the nature of this 'paedagogia eis Christon'; it is sufficient to note here that in Melanchthon's system 'philosophy' and 'law' hold logically parallel positions.[3] Their relation to the Gospel itself finds a striking explanation in a biblical analogy: 'sicut manus Jacob similes sunt manibus Esau, ita Evangelium de vita

[1] Cf. 6, 655; Luther, De Wette, 1, 127 and in his table-talks on Melanchthon's dialectics.

[2] Which yet leaves room for improvements: 'retineo autem plerumque sententias in scholis receptas et usitatam docendi formam, cumque nobis in Ecclesia quaedam paulo aliter dicenda sint, quam dicuntur ab Aristotele, peto mihi veniam dari, si interdum ab Aristotelica phrasi discessi. Vellem sermonis munditiem maiorem esse; non enim sentio has res eleganter dici non posse', CR, 3, 911. See the whole emphasis on 'methodus' and 'perspicuitas', 11, 282; 2, 927; 16, 280; 7, 475, etc.

[3] Cf. CR, 12, 689: 'Philosophia de moribus est ipsa lex Dei de civilibus moribus'; ibid. 691: 'quia Philosophia, quatenus habet demonstrationis, est ipsa lex naturae.'

civili nihil prorsus praecipit aliud, quam quod philosophia et ipsae leges docent. Pomponius Atticus et Paulus Apostolus differunt, quod de Deo dissentiunt. Alter dubitat, utrum Deo curae sit res humanae, et sine Deo vivit; alter certe statuit, quod Deus vere puniat, item, quod ignoscat propter Christum, quod respiciat et audiat. Non dissentiunt in illo genere civilium morum' (12, 689 sq.). Whatever the place of Hellas may be in the light of the revelation [1]—in the realm of ethics we stand on common ground; and this is for Melanchthon the highest practical value of the school of Greece, that it instructs the young in moral philosophy and helps to train responsible citizens.[2] From this Platonic platform it can be seen how the 'concessions to tradition' lead necessarily on to 'reason', 'law' and 'power'.

But in the meantime Melanchthon is not blind to the 'discrimen Christianae doctrinae et Philosophiae' (cf. 16, 280 sqq.) which applies even to the moral sphere; there are two different scales of virtue, centred around 'honesty' and 'fear of God',[3] and there is the ignorance of, and impotence against, original sin in human nature, 'nec Philosophia adversus haec ostendit efficacia remedia... deinde quod etiam remedium adversus illa exhibet, promittit (Deus) enim Spiritum Sanctum' (16, 281). In metaphysics, three fundamental errors are registered: the denial that the government of the world is God's; the statement that civil justice is enough before God; the belief that reason has sufficient power of its own to deal with sin (12, 692 sq.). The final issue is again, as always for Melanchthon,[4] that of certainty; the three 'normae certitudinis iuxta philosophiam: experientia universalis, noticia principiorum, et intellectus ordinis in syllogismo' (13, 150; cf. 186, 647 sq.) are insufficient and point

[1] 'Non enim venit Christus in mundum, ut praecepta de moribus doceret, quae iam ante norat ratio', 16, 280; 'Ineptit etiam Augustinus, qui dicit, se Christianorum doctrinam in Platonicis reperisse, praeter hunc unum articulum: Verbum caro factum est. Recte dixisset Augustinus, si dixisset, eas leges de moribus se reperisse apud philosophos, quae leguntur apud Christianos', 12, 690 sq.

[2] Cf. *CR*, 1, 74: 'ad vitae rationes formandas pertinent'; 11, 283: 'ad mores etiam conducere videtur'; 1, 722: 'ego mihi ita conscius sum, non aliam ob caussam τεθεολογηκέναι nisi ut vitam emendarem.'

[3] 'Cato amat virtutem, sed non propter Deum', 13, 156.

[4] Cf. above, pp. xviii, xxvii and *CR*, 21, 401: 'Hoc eo dicendum est, ut sciamus quid defuerit illis summis viris, Xenophonti, Ciceroni et similibus; norant enim legem et promissiones conditionales legis. Sed quia promissionem gratuitae reconciliationis, hoc est, Evangelium non norant, ideo haesit in eis dubitatio, utrum Deus esset eis placatus, utrum Deus eos exaudiret' (cf. 13, 156).

beyond themselves to the infallible witness of the Holy Spirit: 'in the Church we have a fourth norm of certainty, namely the divine revelation, made through illustrious and infallible testimonies as contained in the prophetic and apostolic writings' (13, 151).

To confound philosophy with Christianity is therefore a fatal mistake, but to reject philosophy is the sign of illiteracy (cf. 16, 280). Between the two popular extremes Melanchthon keeps to the proper course: 'I am not ignoring the fact that philosophy is one kind of doctrine and theology another; neither do I want them both to be mixed, as a bad cook would mix many things together, sed adiuvari Theologum volo in oeconomia methodi. Multa enim mutuari eum ex Philosophia necesse erit' (11, 282; cf. 11, 424; 23, 278). The function of philosophy is like that of the other arts, 'ut ancillae sequantur', and the theologian, availing himself of this offer, must see to it 'that each kind of doctrine is given its proper place' (11, 934); here Melanchthon applies the Pauline ὀρθοτομεῖν τὸν λόγον τῆς ἀληθείας (12, 696; cf. 2 Tim. ii, 15). It was in accordance with this design that Melanchthon's successors developed the 'loci communes' into the dogmatic system of the Lutheran orthodoxy; and to aim at a new type of 'summa theologiae' could not be an offence simply because scholastics had tried to do the same. St Paul's warning, 'lest any man spoil you through philosophy and vain deceit' (Col. ii, 8), is qualified by the appositions 'after the tradition of men, after the rudiments of the world, and not after Christ'; as Melanchthon wittily observes: 'non improbat philosophiam, sed abusum, ut, si quis dicat, cave ne vino decipiaris, is non vituperat vinum sed abusum' (CR, 12, 689). Of the proper philosophy it can truly be said that 'Deus ipse invitat nos ad hanc Philosophiam' (21, 370), and that scripture itself is both the witness to its dignity and the key to its understanding. 'I had never been able to understand the nature and use of philosophy before I came to attain this pure doctrine of the Gospel which in these days through God's singular benefit has been reborn. I believe that many would share this admission and frankly confess that only through the knowledge of the doctrine of Christ they have learnt to perceive the dignity, power and use of philosophy; but now after this dignity has been illustrated and manifested through the Gospel they must be judged as ungrateful in declining to use this benefit of the Gospel and despising these studies which the Holy Spirit greatly commends' (10, 690).

We need not go into further detail. The outline of the concessions thus made to the school of Greece is sufficient to explain Melanchthon's appeal to English theology. For nothing is so typical of the English method as distinct from continental 'Biblicism' as the approach to theological problems from the philosophical angle—in the pulpit no less than in the lecture room. At first sight it seems a puzzle and even a paradox when we consider that the German outlook is supposed to be 'philosophical' and the English purely 'practical'. But it is not a matter of national temper and character. The difference lies in the fact that English theology, in principle and in practice, has preserved the Greek tradition to a far larger extent than is known on the continent. A glance at the syllabus of the universities and training colleges shows the key position occupied by the study of the 'classics' and the 'Fathers' (as well as athletics!); here is the link with antiquity and the Middle Ages which the English Reformation was careful not to destroy and, incidentally, the ground for the instinctive Anglican sympathy with the Eastern Orthodox Church. Of course within this tradition there is room for variety and rival schools; the names of Plato and Aristotle mark the two main streams of thought, and we can obviously not expect people like the Cambridge Platonists to hold a special affection for Melanchthon. Yet they would doubtlessly agree with him when he says 'vera sunt eadem, ubicunque recte traduntur, sive apud Aristotelem, sive apud Platonem' (CR, 13, 658). The common presupposition is that the Greeks have proved right in their concept and quest for 'verity'; they have set the general frame of mind to which the final answer revealed in the Gospel is fitted. Is this to concede too much? And if so, what is the proper measure to limit the sphere of Greek influence? Melanchthon has done enough if he has made us think about the answer, much as it may differ from his own.

B. THE SCHOOL OF ROME

'Vera sunt eadem, ubicunque recte traduntur'—there is a clear emphasis upon the last word. A man of Melanchthon's calibre, just because he has no speculative talent and no genius of originality, must show himself particularly anxious about the 'recte tradere'. Nevertheless, his work is not without a deeper meaning. In handing down to us the burning torch of truth he fulfils a vital function, and he follows the example of the school of Rome, whose merit was not so much the creation of new ideas as the new presentation and systematization of the Greek inheritance. Cicero and Galen stand as mediators between Aristotle and Melanchthon; he reads the Greek classics through Latin spectacles.[1] Similarly, *Christian* Rome is the preparatory school through which he has to pass on his way 'ad fontes' and toward which he feels a lasting debt of gratitude. Even when it comes to the final break with his teachers, he is very far from discrediting or leaving the mother Church; he is at pains to prove that he is in the true ancient tradition: 'vestra est illa, Magistri nostri, non Lutheri theologia, quae a patribus dissentit' (*CR*, 1, 406). The 'school of Rome', then, is not exactly a parallel to the 'school of Greece'; it is not an independent source of knowledge outside the Gospel, but an authorized translation of the Gospel itself, the faithfulness and accuracy of which is at stake. There a philosophy, here an authority is in question; the problem, in Melanchthon's own words, is 'de ecclesia et autoritate verbi Dei' (23, 594 sqq.).

In many ways the 'concessions to Rome' are more acute and evident than those to the school of Greece; not only because of the obvious immediate contact with the Roman Church and the daily necessities of negotiations,[2] but also because of Luther's excessive polemics 'wider das Papsttum zu Rom, vom Teufel gestiftet', which inevitably caused Melanchthon to strike the irenic note. We can hardly be surprised at the frequent efforts to win him back to the 'catholic' Church.[3] His 'traditionalism'[4] disposed him by nature to a promising response. 'Non nova dogmata' was his life-long watchword,[5] 'amor novitatis' his gravest charge against the Anabaptists (*CR*, 25, 223), as well as against the frivolous opinions of Copernicus.[6] Moreover, Me-

[1] Cf. *CR*, 11, 501; and Heinrich Maier, 'Melanchthon als Philosoph', *Archiv für Geschichte der Philosophie*, IX, X, 1909.

[2] See below, Chapter IV B.

[3] See G. Kawerau, *Die Versuche, Melanchthon zur katholischen Kirche zurückzugewinnen*, 1902.

[4] Cf. O. Ritschl, *Dogmengeschichte des Protestantismus*, I, 200 sqq., 278, 289, etc.

[5] 'Extant mea scripta, in quibus non volui gignere nova dogmata, sed dispersam doctrinam in magna varietate disputationum, breviter, ut in schola fieri necesse est, colligere, et quasi σωματοποιεῖν... semper enim Ecclesiae iudicio me subieci', *CR*, 9, 439; 39; 11, 600; 21, 602.

[6] *CR*, 13, 216; see above, p. 6.

lanchthon speaks for the whole Lutheran Church when he declares in the *Apologia Confessionis Augustanae* (Art. III, § 268): 'We know that what we have said agrees with the prophetic and apostolic scriptures, the holy fathers, Ambrosius, Augustine and most others, and with the universal Church of Christ'; the official course has always been 'to check new and ungodly tenets' and therefore to give prominence to the reception in the Lutheran Liber Concordiae of the three oecumenical symbols.[1] Luther himself, in the *Articuli Smalcaldici*, states expressly: 'de his articulis [sc. de summis articulis divinae maiestatis, as contained in the Creeds] nulla est inter nos et adversarios controversia, quum illos utrinque confiteamur.' And Melanchthon lays great stress upon the professed agreement in their views of the early Church: 'Ubi veteris Ecclesiae perspicuam sententiam pii considerabunt, postea secum disputent, an licuerit recentioribus aliam sententiam comminisci. Non contemnendum esse vetustae Ecclesiae consensum statuo, ubi περὶ ῥητοῦ καὶ διανοίας quaestio est.... I have often discussed the sayings of the ancient with Luther himself; and he marvelled how the moderns could dare as much as dissent from antiquity in such a matter, as if they did not audaciously feign other things' (*CR*, 8, 278; cf. 68).

The distinction between 'veteres' and 'recentiores' provides one of the chief arguments against the Papacy and the later Roman tradition, and here again Melanchthon's protest differs from Luther only in tactics, but not in strategy. 'For the Pope says, he wants to hold a Council according to the custom of the Church. But the custom as it is to-day is vastly different from what it used to be in the ancient councils. For in the ancient councils things had to be judged from the Word of God, as we see in Acts xv and elsewhere in the acts of subsequent laudable councils. But afterwards under the Papacy they adopted quite a different method and judged, as is manifest, from their own constitutions and power. Now it is known that we question the constitutions in as far as they are against the Word of God; therefore this matter cannot be decided from the constitutions, but must be judged from the Word of God' (2, 655). This 'judicium de concilio' (1533) is of course of very practical significance; it does not only endorse Luther's weighty admission[2] that 'concilia possunt errare', but

---

[1] See, for example, *Praefatio Electorum, Principum et Ordinum Imperii Augustanae Confessioni Additorum.*

[2] In the disputation with Eck, Leipzig, 1519.

it fixes the Protestant 'conditio sine qua non' as regards participation in any future oecumenical council. How far Melanchthon himself did abide by his principle, is another point.[1] Tradition can never become an autonomous voice of equal authority with the Word of God; to allow this coordination is the heresy of the Council of Trent.[2] Only as commentators of the text of scripture can and must the fathers and councils be consulted;[3] hence we have to distinguish between 'obedire scripturae' and 'amplecti symbola' (*CR*, 9, 279); 'iudicandum est ex verbo Dei, et vetus Ecclesia...consulenda est' (12, 479).[4]

All this is precisely what the twentieth of the Thirty-Nine Articles means by the authority of the Church: 'although the Church be a witness and a keeper of holy Writ, yet, as it ought not to decree any thing against the same, so besides the same ought it not to enforce any thing to be believed for necessity of salvation.' But it leads to a concept of *succession* which is different from, and, in our opinion, more consistent than, the one commonly held to-day by large parts of the Anglican communion. 'Ecclesia aliter se habet. Est enim coetus non alligatus ad ordinariam successionem, sed ad verbum Dei. Ibi renascitur Ecclesia, ubi Deus restituit doctrinam, et dat Spiritum Sanctum. Et hoc modo regi et conservari Ecclesias, non ordinaria successione' (*CR*, 23, 598; cf. Eph. iv, 11 sq.). In other words, to be in the apostolic succession is to continue in the apostles' doctrine; no guaranty of any other kind can be accepted, and no Bishop is exempt from this test. Already the *Apologia Confessionis Augustanae* has reason to complain about the 'religious' people who want to retain apostolic rites without apostolic doctrine (Arts. VII–VIII, § 38). Consequently 'cum Episcopi non recte docent, nihil ad Ecclesiam pertinet ordinaria successio, sed necessario relinquendi sunt' (*CR*, 21, 844). Such an emergency justifies and even demands

---

[1] See below, Chapter IV B.

[2] Cf. Conc. Trid. Sessio IV: 'pari pietatis affectu ac reverentia suscipit et veneratur', Mirbt, *Quellen zur Geschichte des Papsttums und des röm. Katholizismus*, Tübingen, 1934, p. 291.

[3] 'Ut lumen adferrent exempla praeceptis, et ut videri posset, quantum utilitatis adferat haec ars ad intelligendas doctorum hominum disputationes', *CR*, 1, 1080.

[4] *CR*, 15, 1172: 'non est ambiguitas in scriptis Propheticis et Apostolicis, tamen quia in contentionibus etiam plane dicta diversis interpretationibus transformantur in plures sententias, prodest audire testimonia purioris Ecclesiae in aliquis materiis et ea conferre ad fontes, quae cum videmus magis congruere cum fontibus, multum confirmamur et his ipsis testimoniis.'

the segregation of the faithful, however much this step is to be dreaded as a rule (25, 223 sqq.); but it was the emergency which Luther had to face.[1] 'The indispensable correlate to Tradition is Reformation'[2]—'renascitur Ecclesia!'—and just because the Roman Church has failed and still fails to realize that, it became guilty of the schism. Melanchthon, for all his deep regard of 'consuetudo' (cf. CR, 13, 228), could not hesitate to admit 'viciosam consuetudinem non esse ius. Therefore we discontinue your custom, as we know it contradicts the doctrine transmitted by the Son of God, and as it is written in Ezekiel (xx, 18-19): walk in my statutes, not in the statutes of your fathers'.[3]

Church history, therefore, and in particular the period directly preceding the Reformation, must be viewed in a new critical light. The guiding principle is 'that there will always be a Church of God, sometimes more, sometimes less numerous, sometimes more, sometimes less oppressed by errors; etsi Astream poetae dicunt terris expulsam esse, tamen sciamus, Dei vocem de iustitia concionantem nec deleri nec opprimi posse. Et hanc multi furenter contemnunt, tamen semper audiet Ecclesia' (CR, 15, 1393; 2, 853). This presupposes Luther's distinction between the official Church which only bears the name and the true Church which is often found under excommunication and persecution; it also clearly makes the 'vox de iustitia concionans' the decisive mark of the Church. 'These distinctions of vocations are necessary to

---

[1] 'In cases where the Church has to choose between the right Gospel and the rightly interpreted and rightly administered sacraments on the one hand, and, on the other hand, the formal continuity of ordination, she must choose the Gospel and the Sacraments. The Anglican Church has not been faced with this choice. But the Lutheran Churches have been in this situation' (Einar Molland, 'The possibility of a united Christendom from the Scandinavian Standpoint', in Kenneth Mackenzie, Union of Christendom, S.P.C.K. 1938, pp. 446 sq.). The relevant passage in the Apologia to which Molland refers is Art. XIV, §§ 24-25: 'Hac de re in hoc conventu saepe testati sumus, nos summa voluntate cupere conservare politiam ecclesiasticam et gradus in ecclesia, factos enim humana auctoritate. Scimus enim, bono et utili consilio a patribus ecclesiasticam disciplinam hoc modo, ut veteres canones descri-bunt, constitutam esse. Sed episcopi sacerdotes nostros aut cogunt hoc doctrinae genus, quod confessi sumus, abiicere ac damnare, aut nova et inaudita crudelitate miseros et innocentes occidunt. Hae causae impediunt, quo minus agnoscant hos episcopos nostri sacerdotes.'

[2] W. Oelsner, 'Tradition as theological problem', in And other Pastors of Thy Flock, A German Tribute to the Bishop of Chichester, Cambridge, 1942, p. 161.

[3] Acta Wormaciensia, Die xvi Septembris; not in CR.

consider because of the politically minded who wonder why Paul who appears like a vagabond should be more trusted than the Bishops who have the "lawful authority". Here we must note that the Apostles by a singular vocation are sent by God immediately and have unfailing divine testimonies so that their voice must be believed as if God Himself spake from heaven' (15, 1233).[1] It is essential to note the apostles' primacy over all their successors; to them only, in the evangelical concept of tradition, is reserved the character of 'immediacy' and 'infallibility' in their vocation, and the first notion of all true apostolicity is the realization that we are *not* apostles ourselves.[2] On this fundamental point depends the understanding of the whole Reformation doctrine of the Holy Spirit in its opposition to all enthusiasts and prophets of the 'inner light' from Thomas Münzer to Frank Buchman. But even the apostles' authority is, according to Melanchthon, based not on a creative, but on a truly 'traditional' function: 'quia non gignunt ipsi novum genus doctrinae, sed accipiunt certa mandata a Deo, haec sonant et addit testimonia Deus, quod non errent, sicut Moises subinde repetit hoc exordium: Locutus est Dominus Deus' (15, 816). And just because of the significance of this exordium it is impossible to overlook that 'even times near the apostolic age have produced the most awful sects' (15, 1392; cf. 1075), or to deny, on account of the disciples' behaviour in Matt. xv, that 'even in the Apostles there was the error of regarding the discrimination of dishes as singularly important acts of worship.... We should learn from this example not to marvel that there have been some such errors in Augustine, Ambrosius and others. There are always some sins and some ignorance in all men, in some more and in others less' (14, 879). Here again Melanchthon sides with Luther's insistence that the apostles were 'miserable sinners as we are' and against the Roman habit of glorifying their persons while ignoring their doctrine.

[1] Cf. the famous reference that St Paul, according to Gal. i, 11, 12, 16 and ii, 6, was himself not in any 'apostolic succession', in Melanchthon's *Tractatus de potestate ac primatu Papae*, see J. Müller, *Symb. Bücher d. ev.-luth. Kirche*, p. 329, § 10. Also *CR*, 15, 547: 'Apostolus est immediate a Christo vocatus ad docendum Evangelium...ac certum est eum habere Spiritum Sanctum, et in doctrina non errare, ac potest ubique in omnibus Ecclesiis docere. At Episcopus est vocatus per homines ad docendum Evangelium, certo loco, et potest errare, nec necesse est certum esse, quod habet Spiritum Sanctum.'

[2] Cf. Hans Asmussen, 'Ein kleiner Spiegel für das kirchliche Amt', in *Rechtgläubigkeit und Frömmigkeit*, III, Berlin, 1939, p. 95.

'Sed teneatur haec firmissima regula: Impossibile est ullos coetus reiicientes scripta Prophetica et Apostolica esse Ecclesiam Dei' (12, 625). According to this rule tradition must be examined and the more 'prudent' fathers such as Augustine and Bernard (15, 541) be selected from the inferior teachers. No wonder that in particular Augustine appears in Melanchthon's interpretation of Matt. xxii as 'hac veste ornatus' (14, 382) and marks a turning point in Church history: 'Before the times of Augustine, the light of the doctrine of faith was almost extinct, thanks to Origen and Pelagius. Augustine kindled it again, then again it was obscured through the monastic imaginations' (14, 296). And Luther felt sure that Augustine at the reading of Melanchthon's works would repay the compliment: 'Augustinus...gauderet, sed S. Hieronymus...would write against it' (WA Ti, 1, 316; cf. 2, 1842). The line from Augustine to Luther and the parallel between the two 'defensores fidei' need hardly be mentioned; it is reflected in the common prayers of Melanchthon's generation which praise the event of the Reformation as the recovery of the Gospel light from the ages of darkness. Both the Papacy and the Episcopate fall under the same verdict: 'Papa, etsi videri vult retinere libros Propheticos et Apostolicos, tamen et idola manifesta contraria contra legem Dei et dogmata falsa defendit et manifestis mendaciis addit parricidia, ut agnosci possit, regi consilia Pontificia a Diabolo, qui est mendax et homicida' (CR, 12, 625); and the Roman Bishops add to that the fourfold error of (a) assuming the power of instituting new cults; (b) of binding the consciences with deadly sins whenever one of their traditions is violated; (c) assuming the power of interpreting scripture by their own royal authority; (d) assuming the political power of transferring the kingdoms of this world—'hae falsae persuasiones necessario taxandae sunt' (12, 435). On the other hand, the anathema against Servetus is based on the same argument and put with the same force: 'Servetus rixatur cum Ecclesia omnium temporum' (23, 595). It does not matter whether the error is made in the field of 'faith' or of 'order', in the form of addition to, or subtraction from, the Gospel—once the voice of Christ and the witness of His prophets and apostles has been suppressed or removed from the centre, the Church has ceased to be the Church.

From the many references to individual scholastics[1] we quote

---

[1] Albertus Magnus, CR, 11, 537; Occam, 13, 11; Gerson, 16, 111, 113, 131, 248, 406, etc.

only one: 'Nam qui recte loqui student, res intuentur, quibus nomina attributa sunt; e contra, cum sermo novus fingitur, plerunque et res mutantur, ut in Scoti et similium scriptis non sermo tantum corruptus est, sed umbrae rerum seu somnia excogitata sunt, quibus novae appellationes attributae sunt' (7, 475). This criticism is significant, for it shows that the relation between *res* and *nomina* which was at the heart of the great scholastic controversy is the cardinal question for Melanchthon too; his intention is clearly to improve,[1] not to abandon the scholastic tradition, 'cumque seu natura seu fato aliquo ad hanc scholasticam militiam traherer' (4, 716), and once again we touch upon the crucial issue of language in theology. The problem of tradition is the problem of interpretation. 'What is the meaning of these words: I believe one Catholic Church? Does it mean: I believe all the Church says? That surely cannot be accepted without qualification. The truth abides in the Church. And yet many can err. The meaning is rather: I believe that there is and will ever be a Church, i.e. I am sure that Church always is and will remain for ever.... Thou must include thyself in the Church and raise thyself in all perils with this hope and consolation: God will save us and the Church, even if everything seems to be doomed and ruined' (24, 393). In the same way the Creed had been explained in Luther's *Minor Catechism*, by adding the 'pro me' to the objective truths in each of the three articles. 'Debes enim te includere in Ecclesiam' was, in fact, the programme of the Reformation. It was an oecumenical, not a separatistic movement. 'Ac sentis', concludes Melanchthon, 'Ecclesiam Christi esse nostras Ecclesias, et pios ubicunque terrarum iudicio et voluntate cum nostris Ecclesiis coniunctos' (4, 718).

---

[1] *CR*, 2, 925: 'Eamque ob caussam usitatis in Ecclesia verbis usus sum, et interdum a scholis verba quaedam mutatus sum, quae sunt condonanda temporibus. Caeterum dedi operam, ut sermo esset perspicuus. Non admiscui peregrinas disputationes.' See above, p. 7.

CHAPTER II

CONCESSIONS TO REASON

A. NATURAL THEOLOGY

In his *Humanistische Reden und Vorträge*, cited above, W. Jaeger draws attention to the fact that the Romans coined for what they had received from Greece the name 'humanitas'; they did not call it just Greek culture, but human culture.[1] This telling detail of terminology explains by itself why we find it impossible to do without the schools of Hellas and Rome, because what they teach us is no specialist knowledge, but the very elements of 'humanity'. The Graeco-Roman tradition is indeed the cradle of all 'natural theology' in the twofold sense that it embodies 'quod consentaneum est' (*CR*, 13, 244, 228),[2] and that it represents the plea for nature within the scope of revelation. From the formal recognition of that tradition which has provided the framework for all Christian thinking, we now turn to the material claims of 'natural theology' and consider the 'concessions to reason' which result from those made to tradition. The question is whether there is a 'general' revelation as distinct from the 'special' one in the Gospel, and what part the 'vox naturae' has to play in relation to the Word of God.

But before we enter into the very popular and very confused discussion on this subject, it is necessary to make a preliminary inquiry about the motive behind it. What interest—other than the comparative study of religion—has Christian theology in exploring the zone outside the life ἐν Χριστῷ? For Luther and Melanchthon the answer is plain. They have a genuine soteriological interest in the salvation of the heathen, and Melanchthon's sympathy for Cicero is shared by Luther: 'Cicero, a wise and studious man, has done and suffered much. I hope our Lord God will be merciful to him and his like' (*WA Ti*, 3, 3925). And there is every reason for us to turn the reflection on the state of the world ante Christum into practical concern for the pagans of to-day; the problem then presents itself in the missionary terms

[1] Op. cit. pp. 118 sq.
[2] We remember Melanchthon's description of Aristotelian philosophy 'quae quasi est vox naturae', *CR*, 13, 381, and similarly 11, 8; see above, p. 5.

of the Christian approach to the non-Christian world, and under this aspect 'natural theology' did indeed form one of the most important items of the World Missionary Conference at Tambaram-Madras in 1938. In the report of Sections I and V of the conference, Dr H. Kraemer defines the two rival views on the relation between the 'natural' and the 'revealed' as that of 'continuity' and 'discontinuity';[1] to the former, taught by Clement of Alexandria and the adherents of the 'logos spermatikos', Christianity appears as 'fulfilment' of all religions; to the latter, represented by Karl Barth, the term 'fulfilment' is applicable only to the Old Testament while all 'natural religion' is unbelief in the sight of Christ and all human desire broken by His cross. Dr H. H. Farmer in the concluding essay of the same volume has tried to show that the two thoughts are not ultimately irreconcilable: 'Christ is always...both final judge and final fulfilment: in the very process of judging He releases and fulfils; in the very process of release and fulfilment He most searchingly judges' (ibid. p. 180). On the other hand, Dr Kraemer, while maintaining that 'the amount of a-greement and mutual understanding *in regard to this problem* reached in Tambaram, has been appallingly small' (p. 7), feels himself compelled, after having accepted the 'Barthian' position, to ask the question which Barth leaves unanswered: 'were those, who lived under the sway of the non-Christian religions, entirely left to their own devices, or has God also somehow worked in them?' (p. 22).

The New Testament, which it is high time to consult on this point, seems to provide ample evidence on either side, and it may be instructive to group the material in antithetic statements. At first sight, the tenor of Acts xvii sounds to be that of 'fulfilment' and of Rom. i and ii that of 'judgment'; yet it is in Acts xvii that we read of the 'times of ignorance' (vv. 23 and 30), whereas according to Rom. i, 19 'that which may be known of God is manifest' in the Gentiles. Psalm cxxxviii, 8 prays 'forsake not the works of thine own hands', but Rom. i declares twice (vv. 24 and 26) that 'God gave them up'. Again, Christ says (John xv, 22), 'If I had not come and spoken unto them, they had not had sin', and Paul finds (Rom. i, 20; ii, 1) 'that they are without excuse'. Finally, the 'continuity' which is most emphatically granted in Acts xiv, 17: 'He left not Himself without witness' is destroyed by the verdict in Eph. ii, 12, 'that at that time ye were...without God in the world'.

[1] Tambaram Series, vol. 1, Oxford, 1939, pp. 1 sqq.

It would be easy to amplify these examples, and easier still to solve the contradiction by attributing the different statements to different authors and periods; but the times have gone when such methods were deemed sufficient to 'explain' scriptural texts. Even those extreme passages which we have selected all agree in at least two directions: they show that the New Testament as a whole is on Dr Kraemer's side when he writes, 'This has nothing to do *with construing systems of natural theology* or of general revelation, but with respect for facts' (ibid. p. 22); and that it no less strongly endorses Dr Farmer's analysis of 'that awareness of God as One who makes sacred or absolute *demand* which can be discerned in varying form at the heart of the religious life of mankind...that God is actively holding man to Himself even in his disobedience and sin' (pp. 172 and 173, note). But the recognition of this sacred demand in pre-Christian religion leads Paul not to a greater leniency, but to a stricter judgment in his challenge to the heathen; just because 'we are the offspring of God', the imperative is inescapable: 'now He commandeth all men everywhere to repent' (Acts xvii, 30). The whole vindication of 'natural theology' in Rom. i–iii only serves the purpose of accusation; there is no word about creative grace (not even Rom. i, 20 or ii, 4b), but solely 'the wrath of God is revealed from heaven' (Rom. i, 18). This is very different from the common concept of a 'preparatory revelation'; leaving aside, for the moment, the appropriateness of the word 'revelation', we cannot fail to observe that the 'preparation' of the heathen for the Gospel consists merely in their notion of the *law* of nature (Rom. ii, 14).

Now it is precisely here, in Rom. ii, 14, that Melanchthon discovers both link and limit between 'natural theology' and the teaching of the Reformation. 'Quaedam voce Dei tradita sunt, quae etiam natura nota sunt, ut praecepta Decalogi.... Sed cum idem divinitus traditum esse audimus, firmius assentimur. Sunt autem aliae quaedam sententiae divinitus traditae, quae antea prorsus ignotae fuerant omnibus creaturis, ut vox Evangelii de Filio Dei...' (*CR*, 13, 651). He makes the same point in his exegesis of Joh. i, 18, 'no man hath seen God', where he contrasts the incarnation with the 'lex naturaliter nota' (14, 182), and in his coordination of 'philosophy' and 'law'.[1] We are not yet examining the 'inner circle' of Law and Gospel and the 'divisio legum' as described in the Loci;[2] we only mark Melanchthon's

[1] See above, p. 7.   [2] *CR*, 21, 391 sqq.; see below, p. 39.

conclusion that the 'lex naturae' is 'conveniens cum prima et
secunda tabula Decalogi' (*CR*, 21, 712 sqq.), and we think that
it is in accordance both with Scripture and experience. For it
does justice to the 'morale' of the heathen instead of arguing the
Christian case against the non-Christian religions on the moral
level. One can, indeed, be 'as without law' while 'being not
without law to God' (1 Cor. ix, 21). But one cannot in the same
way be 'extra Christum' and yet 'in Christo'. It is one thing to
be responsible to the moral law, and another to be responsive to
the Gospel. To Melanchthon this is quite clear. 'Sciendum est
quid alloquaris in invocatione, et deinde cur et quomodo exaudiat
Deus. Errat enim Ethnica (sc. invocatio) dupliciter, de Essentia
et de voluntate Dei' (*CR*, 15, 1317, 991, 1235). Once again the
final issue between 'natural' and Christian religion is that of
dubitatio versus certitudo: 'Of course the Jews and Gentiles have
their conceptions of God, and even declare that He is good and
merciful. But in the agony of the conscience they become overwhelmed with arguments which bid them despair, because they
do not apprehend the firm and certain promise in which God
offers His free forgiveness' (15, 786).[1]

In our days the distinction between 'invocatio Christiana' and
'Ethnica' seems far less clearly drawn. From the fact of the non-
Christian's moral responsibility we are inclined to deduce the
theory of man's natural responsiveness to Christ. From the
sentence 'there is no difference, for all have sinned' (Rom. iii, 23)
we try to draw the consequence that 'they are all redeemable'.
Especially of English theology it must be said that it is conspicuous
for this tendency. But it is significant that the Bible is equally
conspicuous for its absence. The category of potentiality (re-
deem-able) is scholastic, not scriptural; the offer of the Gospel
to every creature does not open the door to creatural religion;
that man is free in his response is a logical not a biblical implica-
tion.[2] In other words, the interest in the 'vocatio gentium', which
is also manifest in Melanchthon's works, is purely missionary;
'God will have all men to be saved, and to come unto the knowledge of the truth' (1 Tim. ii, 4): 'He has called you out of
darkness into His marvellous light' (1 Pet. ii, 9)—but there is

---

[1] See Luther on Cicero, above, p. 18.
[2] This is also true of the curious insistence that 'God treats us as persons',
to which the biblical reply is: 'there is no respect of persons with God'
(Rom. ii, 11).

simply no room for the abstract reflection on a medium state between darkness and light and on man's character as a 'savable' being. Either he is saved by God's grace alone, or he is lost through his own fault; we must leave it at that, and the great biblical paradox cannot be resolved by ascribing to man a general capacity for redemption, a natural power for good which is released by the 'special revelation'. Beyond the truism that man is no animal we are not allowed to go; and no further concession to 'natural theology' can be made than that which we read in Luther: 'Now Christ bestows upon me his merit, gifts and righteousness by promise which is apprehended by faith alone. Like as if a prince said to me: "come up to my castle, and I will give thee a hundred sovereigns". Of course I am doing a work by going there, but the hundred sovereigns, as a gift, are not given to me by virtue of my going as an effort on my part, but because the prince has promised them to me' (*WA Ti*, 2, 2409).

This example is particularly suitable to illustrate the uselessness of the attempt to make capital of man's move toward God. Of course, man must move; but does the call of the Gospel really leave him time to reflect on his ability? 'When it pleased God... to reveal His son in me... immediately I conferred not with flesh and blood' (Gal. i, 16)! Melanchthon has been less consistent than Luther in avoiding this temptation; he could not altogether resist the inquiry into man's 'freedom' (which the Bible does not answer), and the Lutheran Church firmly repudiated his synergistic moods.[1] However, if 'natural theology' has failed in the context of conversion, it may succeed elsewhere; the material defeat having been admitted, there remains a formal claim still to be considered; the 'continuity' between the 'natural' and the 'revealed', while of no evangelistic value, may yet become a vital interest of 'reason'. On admittedly 'second thoughts' the ominous *Anknüpfungspunkt* (point of contact) may have to be postulated.

It is difficult enough to obtain final clarity on this issue, not only because of the utter silence of the Bible, but also because the Reformers seem to be at variance with each other and even with themselves; no wonder that the confusion is reflected in the camps

---

[1] Cf. *Formula Concordiae*, Art. II, De libero arbitrio (Solida Declaratio), on the 'modus agendi' and on 'Synergists', in J. T. Müller's edition, p. 603, § 61 sq. and p. 606, § 77 sq.

of their modern interpreters.[1] Melanchthon in all his remarks
about the 'imago Dei' maintains the full weight of the fact of
original sin: 'Quodsi natura esset integra, tum vero in hac notitia
luceret Deus et mens hominis praedita magis perspicua notitia,
multo esset illustrior imago Dei' (*CR*, 16, 23; cf. 13, 154). 'Hac
notitia' refers again to the natural law which is born with us.
'For even in this depraved nature, the notion of the law, like
the notion of numbers, is born with us; it is clear that this philosophical and political wisdom which is congruent with God's
law about external actions is not to be condemned' (16, 536;
cf. 214, etc.). But this time we must lay stress not so much on
the congruity with the divine law which we discussed before,[2]
but on the parallel between moral and scientific knowledge.
'Numeri' and 'leges' are interrelated; the 'law' assumes a universal function similar to the one visualized in Kant's epitaph:
'the starry firmament above, and the moral law within me.' 'The
mind by its own light discerns that this proposition is true, certain
and unchangeable: twice four are eight, as much as this statement
is true, certain and unchangeable: adultery is a shame' (2, 850).[3]
It is essential that the two axioms are both 'immota', because
they are ultimately part of a 'tradition' (here lies the root of
Melanchthon's distrust of all revolutions in science and morals),
and 'vera': 'etsi enim procul et per caliginem haec miranda Dei
opera aspicimus, tamen haec quantulacunque cognitio non est
fallax umbra, sed vera ostendit et esse humanas animas, et testimonium eas de Deo certissimum esse' (13, 5; cf. 69). Thus we
are enabled to discover a number of 'testimonia' in the realm of
creation which are 'certa'[4] and of which Melanchthon gives this
important summary: 'Meanwhile there are many errors in many
people, as nothing is more usual to man in this imbecility than
to have falls, deceits, hallucinations. Yet at the same time there
remains the certainty, divinely confirmed, of many propositions.
It is the will of God that life be one thing and death another, that

[1] Cf., for example, Brunner's and Karl and Peter Barth's readings of
Calvin on this point.
[2] *CR*, 16, 171: 'Vera lux rationis in homine insita naturae, congruit cum
lege Dei, sed nunc in hac caligine obscurior est Dei notitia.'
[3] So, by contrast, there is a correspondence in the realm of the Gospel
between the numerical paradox that one is three, and the moral paradox
that the sinner is justified.
[4] 'Non dicas falsum testimonium, inquit vox divina; non delectemur
corruptelis veritatis', *CR*, 2, 850.

there be a certain discrimination of the species, that the appointed orders of generation and nutrition be not violated, that the order of numbers be unchangeable, that the distinction between good and evil be immovable for it is an image of the divine mind. And like as that eternal mind is equal and unchangeable in itself, so the numbers and notions which spring from that source are unchangeable' (13, 188).

Here we are very near to the Thomist doctrine of the 'analogia entis', and it is not incidental that the mind is the organ of continuity. 'Nam imago Dei erat in mente.... Etsi autem post lapsum voluntas aversa est, et in mente notitia obscurior facta est, tamen manet notitia, ut extet aeternum et immutabile iudicium Dei contra peccatum, testificans Deum irasci peccato' (21, 801). However deeply the human will has been corrupted through the fall of Adam, the faculty of the mind has not been destroyed; so the intellect seems to be somewhat less affected by the damage of original sin; reason retains its integrity at least in the process, though not in the aims, of thinking. To underline this last distinction, Melanchthon adds: 'But the promise of reconciliation after the Fall is not a notion inherent in nature, but it is the voice coming out of the secret depths of the father's bosom which before was unknown to any creature' (ibid.; cf. 21, 351; 23, 279; 16, 23). What is left intact in fallen nature is after all but a knowledge unto death rather than unto life;[1] and the emptiness of even formally 'correct' conceptions can be studied from the Platonic description of God: 'God is eternal Mind, the cause of good in nature.... All this Plato has comprehended. But although the cogitations of the human mind, so far as they go, are true, enlightened and born out of firm demonstrations, tamen addendum est, qualem se Deus ipse patefecerit' (21, 610).[2]

'Addendum' is a highly dangerous word to be used in this connection. For the one concession which it would be absolutely fatal to make is to believe that Plato knew the first article of the Christian Creed and only wanted the special revelation of the second. This is the cardinal error of 'natural theology',[3] it is a

---

[1] 'Ut extet aeternum iudicium Dei contra peccatum', see above.

[2] *CR*, 6, 654: 'Nam normae illae [sc. quae κριτήρια vocantur], experientia, principia, intellectus consequentiae, sunt revera vox divina; et his addimus doctrinam ecclesiae divinitus traditam.' See above, p. 8.

[3] 'Melanthon retulit Lutherum saepe dixisse articulum de remissione peccatorum esse fundamentum, unde extruatur articulus de creatione', *WA Ti*, 4, 4857 h.

deadly sin against the trinitarian faith, and Melanchthon shows himself aware of it when he chooses to speak of the 'Logos spermatikos' in the subjunctive: 'Itaque sicut Sol lucem et calorem in hoc aere spargit, ita Deus in mentes nostras sparsisset λόγον et Spiritum Sanctum. Ac λόγος monstrasset patrem, et multiplici sapientia mentes illustrasset, voluntates autem et corda copulasset Spiritus Sanctus aeterno patri, mutuo amore, laeticia et motibus congruentibus cum natura Dei. Such would have been the human wisdom and life, in concord with the wisdom and life of God. And these goods, lost in the Fall, are being restored through the Gospel' (13, 154).

But having averted this danger, we are still suspiciously near to Thomas Aquinas when we survey Melanchthon's catalogue of 'iudicia providentiae' in the chapter of the Loci 'de creatione' (21, 641 sqq.; 13, 200 sqq.) and when we hear even Luther declare: 'reason does not grasp what God is, but it most certainly grasps what he is not.'[1] Can the 'formal' 'imago Dei in mente' really be carried as far as that? Does this not leave a far too big share to 'reason' and open the field for all the ill-famed proofs of the existence of God? Is the 'esse Dei' evident to science and only the 'essentia' accessible to faith?

Luther himself said very firmly No to these suggestions when in his *Disputatio de sententia: Verbum caro factum est*[2] he denounced the thesis of the Sorbonne 'quod etiam vera sint in theologia, quae in philosophia vera sunt, et e contra'. Following St Paul's advice to 'bring every thought into captivity to the obedience of Christ', he wants to silence the voice of philosophy in the Church—quoting 'mulier taceat in ecclesia'—and accuses his opponents of putting new wine into old bottles (see Theses 8, 14, 41). He illustrates from syllogistic and scientific examples that 'aliquid est verum in una parte philosophiae, quod tamen falsum est in alia parte philosophiae' (Th. 36), and the supreme instance is the incarnation (itself): 'non quidem vitio formae

---

[1] 'Non enim capit ratio, quid sit deus, certissime tamen capit, quid non sit deus. Ita licet non videat, quid rectum et bonum sit coram deo (nempe fidem), scit tamen evidenter infidelitatem, homicidia, inobedientiam esse mala.' After quoting Mark iii, 24 and 1 Cor. xi, 14 for the use of 'reason' by Jesus and Paul, Luther concludes: 'quod ergo huic rationi evidenter adversatur, certum est et deo multo magis adversari. Quomodo enim coelesti veritati non pugnabit, quod terrenae veritati pugnat?' This is proved from John iii, 12. The passage is found in *WA*, VIII, 629, 23 sqq.

[2] Drews, *Disput.*, Göttingen, 1896, pp. 485 sqq.

syllogisticae, sed virtute et maiestate materiae, quae in angustias rationis seu syllogismorum includi non potest' (Th. 20). Hence his life-long struggle against the 'harlot reason', the inevitable outcome of which seems to be a final dualism in the concept of truth.

Have we then to submit to the idea of a 'doppelte Wahrheit'? Even if we could bear it, the question would remain [1] what value— other than mere technicality—there is in scientific and philosophical research in the sight of God; what has His Word to say about man's quest for truth? Even Luther in the context of the above-quoted disputation cannot help using such terms as 'eundum ergo est ad aliam dialecticam et philosophiam in articulis fidei, quae vocatur verbum Dei et fides' (Th. 27); and Melanchthon in his earliest anti-philosophic mood demands 'philosophiam purgabimus, ut apti accedamus ad theologica' (CR, 1, 50). It is a genuine Christian desire to discover the true relation between the certainty of 'twice four are eight' and that of the Gospel; to practise in the sphere of abstraction the command 'thou shalt love the Lord thy God with all thy mind'; to reconcile the enmity between reason and revelation. This is what Hegel intended with his distinction of 'Verstandsreflexion' and 'Vernunft als Vernehmen des göttlichen Werkes'.[2] Why should not the 'harlot reason' become converted? Here we return to our original missionary viewpoint in a new sense. Of course, conversion may not, or not fully, be achieved in this fallen world, and the purge of philosophy which Melanchthon planned may point to an eschatological purgatory. In any case it remains of the greatest importance that St Paul in 1 Cor. xiii, 9 sq. 'does not say that the preliminary knowledge will be entirely destroyed, but rather that imperfection will cease and an obscure, shadow-like knowledge, intermixed with doubts, will become a lucid and immovable one, et ut vocabulis notis utamur, ex abstractiva fiet intuitiva, plena lucis et splendoris. Ut si quis aliquem in crepusculo utcunque conspectum, postea in clara luce mani-festius intuetur' (CR, 15, 1145).[3]

---

[1] Parallel to the one put by Kraemer to Barth, see above, p. 19.

[2] Rational reflection, and spiritual reception of the work of God.

[3] CR, 13, 75 sq.: 'Ingens autem et haec utilitas est, arte considerata ratiocinari, hoc mirandum opus non casu ita confluxisse, nec tamen ad hunc usum in vita mortali conditum esse. Esse etiam arcanam causam, cur ipse filius Dei induerit humanam naturam. Hunc in omni aeternitate tuis oculis intueberis, audies auribus tuis disserentem de sapientia divina, tuo complexu

B. PURE DOCTRINE

Our next task in passing over to 'pure doctrine' is to translate the 'concessions to reason' to another plane. In 'natural theology' reason figured as an independent and rival partner of revelation; in 'pure doctrine' it becomes an element within the realm of revelation itself. This transition is again very largely a matter of theological language, as Luther in the disputation significantly observes: 'Rectius ergo fecerimus, si dialectica seu philosophia in sua sphaera relictis discamus loqui novis linguis in regno fidei extra omnem sphaeram' (Th. 40). Luther obviously thinks of the prophetic ministry in the first instance; while Melanchthon, more familiar with the tongues of men than with those of angels, would apply the 'loqui novis linguis' to the teaching function of the Church. What changes, we wonder, does the kerygma of the Reformation undergo in the process of being defined and established as 'pure doctrine'? And what part does 'reason' play in the act of purification?

At this point it will be helpful to have a look at, though not a full discussion of, certain suggestions made by Dr Temple in his Gifford Lectures [1] in order to find a way out of the deadlock in the traditional interpretation of 'natural theology'. First, 'the false distinction between Natural and Revealed Religion or Theology, which bases the contrast on their contents instead of on the method of handling those contents' (p. 19), is replaced by the new definition 'we understand by Natural Theology the scientific study of Religion' (p. 18). Second, 'Unless all existence is a medium of Revelation, no particular Revelation is possible...for the conditions of the possibility of any revelation require that there should be nothing which is not revelation' (p. 306). Third, 'All therefore is alike revelation; but not all is equally revelatory of the divine character.... There is no such thing as revealed

ipsum salutabis. Tunc demum intelligemus, et cur haec corpora sic condita sint, et quae sit substantia singularum partium. Interea hanc sapientiam utcunque inchoemus, agnoscamus hanc naturam non casu ex Democriti atomis conflatam esse, celebremus Deum architectum, fateamur radios sapientiae divinae in nos non frustra sparsos esse, qui monstrant ordinem omnium actionum, et eis obtemperemus, petamus et expectemus immortali-tatem. Et sciamus tunc demum haec nostra corpora habitura ultimum et perfectum decus, cum coram cernent et audient filium Dei, et undique in eis fulgebit lux divina.'

[1] *Nature, God and Man*, London, 1934 and 1940.

truth.... What is offered to man's apprehension in any specific Revelation is not truth concerning God, but the living God Himself' (pp. 315, 317, 322). Fourth, 'The false estimate of conceptual thinking held by Greek and Scholastic and Cartesian philosophers' (p. 316) which leads to the dilemma of the mind isolating itself from the Universe, must be overcome in a new 'synthesis of the classical and mediaeval "thesis" with the modern "antithesis"' (p. 78).

Most of these statements fall under the heading of the philosophy of religion with which we are not directly concerned here; it remains to be seen whether (ad 1) the scientific approach to revelation can justifiably take the place of the 'regional' division between 'natural' and 'revealed', whether (ad 2) the 'possibility' of revelation is a legitimate theological category (cf. above, p. 21), and whether (ad 4) the readjustment of 'mind' in the new, post-Cartesian and post-Kantian 'synthesis' will account more properly for the effects of original sin in man's 'reflection'.[1] What is clear beyond any doubt, however, is the inescapable necessity for us of applying the Reformation principle of 'Sola fide' to the sphere of thought; and on this point the third of the four above suggestions has the most direct bearing. For the problem of 'pure doctrine' is indissolubly connected with that of 'revealed truth'. H. Asmussen illustrates the importance of Dr Temple's statement that 'there is no such thing as revealed truth' from a rather different angle when he protests against 'a certain interpretation, since the sixteenth century, of truth and doctrine which for the sake of truth and doctrine we must question. This interpretation is determined by the *intellektuelle Werkerei* of which we have already spoken. Doctrine and truth appear as objects in our possession and at our disposal.'[2] *Werkerei der Lehre* is the exact parallel to 'righteousness by works' in the intellectual sphere. It is to rationalize the Gospel instead of evangelizing reason—a charge which none of Luther's opponents, be he 'Papist' or 'Enthusiast', could ever escape and of which in due course Lutheran Orthodoxy itself became guilty. Our question is how far already Melanchthon advanced in this direction.

[1] Cf. above, p. 24 and the important observations on the 'cor curvum in se' in Luther's commentary on Romans (ed. Ficker, 1908, Scholien, ii, 137, 1).
[2] In *Abendmahlsgemeinschaft?*, München, 1937, p. 12.

One obvious safeguard is his ever-repeated distinction between *notitia* (*fides historica*) and *fides* (*fides fiducialis*). 'Fides significat non solum adsentiri historiis, sed etiam promissionibus Dei.'[1] The corresponding distinction on the objective side is between *ratio* and *spiritus*. 'It is certain that the Spirit of God in these passages [sc. Rom. viii, 14 etc.] does not denote reason, as some rash philosophers interpret it, but the Holy Spirit proceeding from the Father and our Lord Jesus Christ, sent into the hearts of the faithful and moving them through the voice of the Gospel to the knowledge of God and to actions conforming to His law' (*CR*, 23, 279). And the limitations of reason can be described even by Melanchthon in terms strangely suggestive of Goethe:[2] 'Nunc ei obtemperemus, agnoscamus discrimen inter naturas ratiocinantes et non ratiocinantes, et Deum celebremus sapientiae fontem, et hoc domicilium reverenter tueamur, quantum possumus. Plura de hoc mirando opificio dicere non possum' (13, 71; cf. 69). Certainty—we had to expect this final turn—is only in the Word, and 'extra verbum nulla revelatio': 'These words of the Son He wants us to believe, and not to seek after other doctrines or illuminations' (15, 339; cf. 430, 785). As with Luther, the polemic is aimed as much at the 'philosophers'[3] as at the 'enthusiasts': 'Why look out for miracles and uncommon examples? Although many of these occur to individuals, yet you should fix your eyes upon the word and wait for that which it promises. In such exercises it will be learnt what is faith' (14, 384).

Yet Melanchthon is very far from any *sacrificium intellectus*. '*Discitur*, quid sit fides.' After all, the notional element in faith is not negligible, and beside the distinction there is also the definite correlation between *notitia* and *fides*: 'There is no knowledge without the light of the word, no faith without promise' (15, 106). Granted that the divine revelation is a communication from person by person to person—'no one knoweth who the Father is but the Son, and he to whom the Son will reveal Him'— still there is an objective 'message' implied in this act: 'blessed are the eyes which see the things that ye see' (Luke x, 22–3); and though

---

[1] *CR*, 13, 166; cf. *Apol. Conf. Aug.* Art. III, p. 150, § 262 (J. T. Müller's edition), and numerous references in the Lutheran Confessions of Faith.

[2] 'Darum ist es das schönste Glück des denkenden Menschen, das Erforschliche erforscht zu haben, und das Unerforschliche ruhig zu verehren', *Jubiläumsausgabe*, 39, 100.

[3] 'Non vult nos sequi humanas imaginationes...sed alligat nos ad verbum Evangelii', *CR*, 15, 188.

the believer trusts in Christ and not in creeds, the teacher has to undertake the proper presentation and explanation of these 'things', and it is to this secondary, but indispensable, task that Melanchthon was called.[1] If true faith is to be established, 'pure doctrine' must needs be defined.

'Deinde nos, quibus doctrinae explicatio commendata est, studeamus concordiam et consensum Ecclesiarum nostrarum tueri' (CR, 6, 92), writes Melanchthon after Luther's death, comparing the situation to that of the 'orphans' in John xiv, 18; it is anything but thrilling—for himself and for his readers—to belong to the second generation of the homines scholastici, grammatici et philosophi,[2] and to have to be on the defensive all the time;[3] in order to preserve the pure milk of the Gospel he has to keep it in tins. And he knows well enough that 'nullus autem libellus est integer aut absolutus' (CR, 4, 719). He cannot go to extremes and he cannot afford the vigour of Luther; his aim must be comprehensiveness for the sake both of the unity of the Lutheran Church and the coherence of its doctrinal system. 'Nos totum doctrinae corpus toties repetivimus, et magna cura exposuimus' (9, 91) is his decisive claim against 'illa turba Flaciana'[4] and against such heretics as Schwenckfeldt.[5] This implies an utter faithfulness to the letter of the Confessio Augustana (7, 605), 'simpliciter et fideliter recitare voluimus, ac repetimus sententiam Confessionis' (8, 49), and the admission 'unde et quidam fastidiunt, me eandem cantilenam canere' (9, 39). Which reader of, for example, the Apologia could ever escape this impression? But the vice turns out to be a virtue 'propter adolescentiam' (ibid.), and even in general 'it was desirable, that the Church should have handed

---

[1] Cf. Dr Temple, op. cit. p. 322.
[2] Cf. CR, 9, 19 and O. Ritschl, Dogmengeschichte des Protestantismus, II, 353, note 1.   [3] See above, pp. xi and xxvi.
[4] CR, 9, 628: 'for it is no help to poor miserable Christendom, that Illyricus (Flacius) here and there objects, that this, that and the other are inadequately said; while he produces no proper corpus doctrinae so that nobody knows what he thinks and where he tends.'
[5] Kaspar Schwenckfeldt, with Karlstadt and Zwingli 'the third head of the pernicious sacramentarian sect' and as such rejected by Luther and the Formula Concordiae for his spiritualistic and anabaptist heresies. He, in Melanchthon's words, 'makes use of the common trick of not publishing a whole body of Christian doctrine of which one could lay hold, as is the duty of a true Christian teacher, but he hides in his corner and filches little bits of our doctrine which he criticizes for the purpose of creating divisions', CR, 8, 562; cf. 12, 198; 11, 899.

down the same matters with even the same syllables, and is still doing so' (8, 274); under the same aspect the extensive use of dialectics is justified by the didactic character of Melanchthon's whole theology (cf. 6, 657).

All this is a process of vital importance for us to watch, as we have arrived at a very similar turn in the development of our own contemporary theology. Only an 'enthusiast' could deplore Barth's step from the 'prophetic' pathos of the *Römerbrief* to the solid positions of the *Dogmatik*; it was the only possible way from chaos to order, and the course towards the 'corpus doctrinae' is fundamentally sound.[1] But we seem to have reached the point where the danger becomes acute that our orthodoxy, like that of Melanchthon, might degenerate into 'canere eandem cantilenam' and thus die from sterilization; large sections of theological publications lose interest in the same measure as they gain uniformity in type; a kind of 'normal' theology dominates the field which is correct but boring and mistakes homiletic exhortations for dogmatic scholarship. The distinctive functions of teaching and preaching suffer from being commonly confused— it is safe to say that the former has deteriorated as much as the latter has improved in Germany—and here again the problem of language deserves our full attention as we read: 'Nec gignit Ecclesia novam doctrinam sed velut Grammatica est sermonis divini; docet teneram aetatem, quid vocabula significent, et distribuit et numerat utcunque membra doctrinae.... Eamque ob caussam initio Symbola condita sunt, ut summa doctrinae in conspectu esset recitata propriis verbis, ut iisdem syllabis hae res praecipue ubique in Ecclesiis praeponerentur' (7, 576, 578). It is proper and inevitable in wartime that the censor should rigorously control the press, and all historical 'confessions' from the Apostles' Creed down to the Barmen declaration express this sense of control on the part of the Church in regard to its own preaching; but while without such 'regulae fidei' the Church struggle would be lost and the pulpit given to anarchy, it would yet be wrong to narrow the scope of the 'corpus doctrinae' to the merely censorial office of guarding and preserving the 'depositum fidei'. 'Pure doctrine' as a chiefly *defensive* concern falls short of the fullness of the Gospel.

The same 'catholic' criticism arises from the material aspect of Melanchthon's—and, indeed, of Luther's—system. What

[1] See above, p. 9.

Jonas reports in Luther's table-talks,[1] has become the traditional charge against the Reformation: that it selected certain one-sided passages from Scripture and presented them as the whole truth, thus effecting a 'rationing' of the Word of God in substance, which, like the censorship in style and method, is justifiable as a wartime measure in critical periods of Church history, but disastrous if made permanent. Luther had found his way to the Gospel through 'Paulinism' and to Paul through Augustine, and Melanchthon's Loci in their concentration on the antithesis of 'Law' and 'Gospel' truly reflect this approach (cf. *CR*, 24, 392). 'Collegi in duobus libellis, in Locis Theologicis et in commentario Epistolae ad Romanos, doctrinam Ecclesiarum nostram.'[2] Whence and why this emphasis on Paul? 'Neither the prophecies of the prophets nor the stories of the Gospels are accessible unless his commentaries are followed methodically, like a stream leading to the ocean.... Neque enim Christum novisse, est historiam rerum ab ipso gestarum tenere, sed agnoscere eius beneficia.... It is in vain to devote thyself to the divine laws unless, under the tutorship of Paul, Christ is recognized as He whom we must implore for the spirit which loves the commands of the law.... In vain hast thou learnt the Gospel story if thou hast not learnt to observe, with Paul, its scope and its use' (11, 38). Thus the Pauline Epistles offer the key to a harmonious and comprehensive interpretation of Gospel, Law and Prophets; far from being on a 'side-track', they reveal most clearly of all the unity of Holy Scripture, and to make Paul the chief 'magister' and 'commentator' in all exegetic studies is the surest way to avoid the obvious danger of dogmatism which we met at the beginning of this chapter.[3] For the Apostle's basic doctrine is not an 'objective truth' about Christ, but the personal application of His benefits. 'Agnoscere eius beneficia' is one of Melanchthon's fundamental definitions of 'fides fiducialis'. The point of his recommendation of Paul is therefore supremely practical: 'when it comes to stablishing and consoling the conscience, nobody, in my opinion, is preferable to Paul' (11, 38). And this is asserted in unusually strong words against alternative suggestions: 'Non

---

[1] 'Ego aliquando audivi ex Philippo, quod tota scriptura nihil aliud sit quam certamen serpentis et seminis', *WA Ti*, 5, 5585.

[2] *CR*, 4, 716; cf. the description of Paul's Epistle to the Romans as 'doctrinae Christianae compendium', 21, 85, 49, etc.

[3] See above, p. 28.

nego esse locos, quibus adflictam conscientiam consoleris et in reliquis scripturae voluminibus, sed subobscuros, et quorum nullus usus futurus erat, nisi a Paulo illustrati essent.... Reliquas artes omneis vel contemnere licet: Paulina, nisi spem omnem salutis abiiecisti, negligi non possunt' (11, 40). In fact, the proportion of non-Pauline and Pauline writings in Melanchthon's view is very similar to that of scripture and tradition in the Roman Catholic Church; without Paul the rest of the Bible appears 'subobscurus'.

If this is wrong, it must be rectified through the New Testament itself, and the first question will have to be whether it is a true interpretation of Paul. The logical completion of the 'Solifidianism', as Wesley used to call it (*Works*, vol. 1, p. 186), lies in the direction of 'good works', and Melanchthon's own schoolmasterliness leads inevitably to a reconsideration of 'Law and Gospel' from the pedagogical angle. Thus the 'concessions to law' follow both from the so-called 'material principle' of the Reformation—justification by faith—and from its 'formal principle' of scripturalness; the material and formal purity of doctrine demands as its outcome and counterpart a doctrine of purity.

CHAPTER III

CONCESSIONS TO LAW

A. THE PEDAGOGICAL ASPECT

Melanchthon regards the task of relating the 'sola gratia' of the Gospel to the discipline of the Law as a practical measure of pastoral theology. 'Iam additur alia admonitio, quod doctrina libertatis non sit tradenda iis, qui nondum sunt recte instituti... volebant omnes laetari cum sponso, et non erant apud sponsum; omnes sumus tales.... Ego respondi: Lutherum tradere doctrinam dextra, sed illos accipere sinistra' (*CR*, 25, 530). The history of the early years of the Reformation has already proved to him how easily the newly won liberty is 'used for an occasion to the flesh', and it is from this experience that the *Unterricht der Visitatoren* was written. If people will play with the good news of the Gospel, they must hear the bad news of the Law; after the first period when the broken in heart were to be healed the time has now come to shake up the hardened sinners (cf. Drews, *Disput.* p. 422). Under these circumstances Melanchthon cannot hesitate to decide 'quod doctrina libertatis non sit tradenda'. But can any emergency justify such a drastic order? Does it not mean the final suspension of the 'articulus stantis et cadentis ecclesiae'? Are not thus the bold principles of Luther sacrificed to the timid counsel of his *epigoni*? This was the critical question asked by Agricola and his friends, and as their protest, caused by Melanchthon's *Articuli Visitatorii*, was meant as an appeal to the 'real' Luther, we must turn to consult Luther himself in his *Disputations against the Antinomians*.

The three disputations (of December 1537, January and September 1538) mark three stages in the relations between Luther and Agricola; in tenor and content they move from friendly adjustment to firm rejection and final break. We may summarize the main arguments as follows: (1) The first disputation is about the two parts of penitence, 'dolor de peccato' and 'propositum bonum' (cf. Drews, p. 253, Th. 4); the former is worked by the Law, the latter by the Gospel; the Scholastic error is to ignore the second, the Antinomian error to abolish the first, or, in either case, to confuse the order. (2) The second disputation is about the twofold purpose of the Law; while it is impotent 'ad iustificationem', it has the vital function to reveal man's sin and God's wrath and to be fulfilled through Christ in the Christians. 'Quare lex nunquam in aeternum tollitur, sed manebit vel implenda in damnatis, vel impleta in beatis' (ibid. p. 339, Th. 47). (3) The third disputation is about the duration of the Law; we are bound to it as long as we live in the body, for 'haec tria, lex, peccatum, mors sunt inseparabilia' (ibid. p. 423, Th. 7), and we cannot know Christ without knowing 'quid sit lex et plenitudo eius' (Th. 62). But we are free from the Law as far as we are already dead to the world and alive with the risen Lord (Th. 36–41); the fatal mistake of Agricola is to anticipate that state of perfection in his followers, 'nam hoc est aliud nihil, quam omnes auditores eorum putare ex hac vita sublatos esse' (Th. 31).

Thus the Antinomian heresy, like every other,[1] is proved guilty of the cardinal sin of 'enthusiasm'; it does not only dispense the Christian from the Law, but it must ultimately lead to the dismissal of the Old Covenant as a failure on the part of God.[2] Law and Gospel appear in the historical order of past and present,[3] whereas the proper position held by the Reformers is 'tota scriptura alias lex, alias evangelium' (CR, 21, 139, 142). Luther, after a first attempt to mediate and to grant to Agricola the benefit of using another terminology,[4] fully endorses Melanchthon's statement: 'quicquid ostendit peccatum, iram seu mortem, id exercet officium legis, sive fiat in veteri sive in novo testamento'.[5] And this usus elenchticus[6] must logically precede the proclamation of the absolution: 'repent ye, and believe the Gospel' (Mark i, 15).[7] So it had been preached in Wittenberg from the very beginning; Melanchthon merely recorded in technical terms what had been the decisive and saving experience of his master; and that experience itself conformed exactly to the Pauline witness of 'repentance toward God, and faith toward our Lord Jesus

[1] See Luther's verdict on the Papacy in the Articuli Smalcaldici, Part III, Art. VIII.

[2] Cf. G. Kawerau, Johann Agricola, Berlin, 1881, pp. 135, 142 f.

[3] Ibid. pp. 176 ff.   [4] See Kawerau, p. 148; cf. p. 173, note 3.

[5] Drews, Disput. p. 337, Th. 18.

[6] The 'tres usus legis' of the Lutheran dogmatics have been translated by A. R. Vidler in Christ's strange Work (Longmans, 1944) as follows: 'God's Law as means of preservation', 'God's Law as summons to repentance', 'God's Law as guidance to the Church'. On the 'tertius usus' see below, p. 42.

[7] Drews, Disput. p. 225, Th. 34; see Kawerau, pp. 175, 185, 221, note 2.

Christ' (Acts xx, 21). The 'real' Luther sides with Melanchthon, and in the end it is Melanchthon's mediation that Agricola, fallen into disgrace, fled to Berlin and forced to recantation, must invoke—in vain—to be restored to Luther's favour.[1]

But at this very point the case must be reopened. Granted that Luther had the overwhelming strength of a Damascus experience to bring against Agricola, did it then follow that the method of evangelization throughout the Lutheran Church was henceforth tied to this pattern? Could not Agricola also quote such texts as this, that 'the people of Nineveh (a) believed God and (b) proclaimed a fast and put on sackcloth' (Jonah iii, 5), and even from St Paul that 'the goodness of God leadeth thee to repentance' (Rom. ii, 4)?[2] If the simple 'abolition' of the Law is out of the question—and in practice, despite the denunciations of his enemies, Agricola never doubted that[3]—the problem of its proper *place* does still remain. One has only to recall the two entirely different settings of the Decalogue in the Lutheran and Heidelberg Catechisms[4] to illustrate the relevance of this debate. G. E. Phillips's *Old Testament in the World Church* (Lutterworth Press, 1942) is another case in point, presented from the experience of the mission field. 'If they are to find the living God, what has happened to the Jews must happen to them in one form or another. The process of religious education cannot be omitted; they cannot pass in one leap from pre-Jewish paganism to knowledge of the God and Father of our Lord Jesus Christ' (p. 135). The danger to the 'infant church' is that some 'teachers give it the Gospel without first giving it the Law, and are surprised that it interprets the Gospel as if it were a law' (p. 96). On the other hand, it may have to be recognized what a convert from Hinduism states 'that the Old Testament comes to a convert later in his Christian life and not before' (p. 14). But in either case 'they must, as soon as they can bear to, seek in the Old the means of truer understanding of the New, and when they return to the New they will find it infinitely richer than when they read it alone. After that they will always think of both together, which is the only right way of reading the Bible'

---

[1] Cf. Kawerau, pp. 197 sq.
[2] Cf. Kawerau, pp. 147, 175.
[3] Cf. Kawerau, pp. 136 ff., 162 ff., 183 ff.
[4] A difference curiously enough reflected in the development of Agricola's own writings from the 'Lukaskommentar' to the '130 Fragstücke' (see Kawerau, pp. 131–42).

(p. 139). Again, the same polarity occurs in the preaching of the Wesleys: should evangelization make its appeal to the 'desire to be saved from sins and to flee from the wrath to come' or should the approach be made solely from 'the love of Christ constraining us'? Both methods are, in fact, found side by side, and it is impossible to turn them into a final alternative or to give a general ruling.

The Wesleyan example is worth being studied in this connection because the parallel with Melanchthon goes further still. In the Moravians Wesley had met the Antinomian version of Lutheranism, and his arguments against Count Zinzendorf follow, without acknowledgment, precisely the line of Luther and Melanchthon against Agricola. One obvious common feature of the two controversies is Wesley's insistence upon the *degrees* of justifying faith;[1] this is in full accordance with Luther's famous statement that 'this life is not being godly but becoming godly; not being whole, but becoming whole; not a status but a process, not a rest but an exercise...' (*WA*, VII, 337, 30), and it is on this very ground that Melanchthon as early as in the first edition of his *Loci* (*CR*, 21, 206) bases the indispensable part of the Law in the divine economy: 'Et leges praescribuntur fidelibus, per quas spiritus mortificet carnem. Nondum enim consummata in nobis libertas est, sed vindicatur, dum et augescit spiritus et necatur caro.' Consequently, the Means of Grace, as the great Standard Sermon reminds us, are all-important in Wesley's concept of sanctification, whereas in the Moravian view 'if a Man regards Prayer, or searching the Scriptures, or Communicating, as Matters of Duty...he is in Bondage, he has no Faith at all, but is seeking Salvation by Works of the Law'.[2] It goes without saying which side stands in the true Lutheran succession. The charge which from the days of Wesley down to Harnack has been brought against Luther and which it is customary to repeat in almost every English handbook on the subject, namely, that he neglected the command 'be ye holy, for I am holy', is, so far from affecting the Reformer, found to be his own old complaint against the Antinomians: 'Thus do my Antinomians, they preach very beautifully and, as I cannot doubt, with great earnest about

[1] See *A short view of the difference between the Moravian Brethren, lately in England, and the Rev. Mr John and Charles Wesley*: 'that there are Degrees in Faith, and that a Man may have some Degree of it, before all things in him are become new.' [2] Ibid.

the grace of Christ, forgiveness of sins and other articles of redemption. But the consequence they flee like the Devil: to tell people of the third article, that is, of the new life in Christ' (*WA*, L, 599, 5 sq.). Those who still mistake the pietist doctrine of 'stillness' (which was rightly opposed by Wesley) for the Lutheran theology of the third article had better be referred to the plain language of the Minor Catechism: 'that I should live under Him in His kingdom and serve Him in eternal righteousness, innocence and bliss', and 'where the Word of God is taught purely and properly and we live accordingly in holiness as God's children'. The words sound almost perfectionist! 'Perfectio Christiana est opus a Deo praeceptum', we read in Melanchthon (*CR*, 12, 698).

Of course there is a point here at which the Wesleys and the Reformers part company and to which we shall have to turn in the next chapter. But they are at one in their emphatic endorsement of the Pauline claim: 'Do we then make void the law through faith? God forbid; yea, we establish the law' (Rom. iii, 31).[1] Melanchthon neatly explains 'that in a threefold way the law is established by faith: first, by the confession of the truth, that God's law justly judges and condemns us; secondly, by the recognition, that the law is not an idle murmur, but that the penalty must be paid; thirdly (reference to Gal. v, 5), those reconciled by faith shall possess the "iusticia integra" which is signified by the law' (*CR*, 15, 883). He tries to meet the objection 'utrum Christus sit legislator?'—apparently mindful of Luther's warning not to make of Christ 'another Moses'—by a subtle trinitarian distinction: 'Christus non est legislator in praesenti sua vocatione, sed tota divinitas est legislatrix. Officium Christi est singulare officium, et tamen est interpres legis' (25, 776). A far more determined and convincing answer to the same question occurs on the previous page: 'Num potest lex tolli? Non: quia Deus non potest tolli' (25, 775).

So we are free, as Wesley would have said, from the curse, not from the rule, of the law.[2] Again, Melanchthon defines four degrees of Christian liberty: 'first: gratuitous remission and re-

[1] Cf. Wesley's sermon, *Works*, v, 447 sq.

[2] Cf. however, by contrast, Luther's commentary on John iii, 34: 'Who believes in Christ, becomes partaker of this immeasurable freedom, where the Spirit says: Thou art free *not only* from the law of Moses, *but also* from all its accusation and condemnation' (*WA*, XLVII, 196, 27).

conciliation. The second degree is the deliverance of the heart
from the infernal pains. These are the two principal degrees (there
follows a reference to John viii, 36). The other degrees concern
external matters. Third: that it is not necessary for a Christian
man to keep the polity of Moses, but he can follow the honest
polities of those people among whom he lives. The fourth degree
is to know that no man-made traditions in the church are part of
divine worship' (14, 829; cf. 15, 722 sq.; 23, 82 sq.). In many
disputations 'de abrogatione legis', 'de libertate Christiana', 'de
usu libertatis in adiaphorois et scandalo', this theme is followed
up (12, 469–78). In order to safeguard the Lutheran concept
of 'freedom from the law' against the erroneous Antinomian
consequences it is necessary to divide the 'law' according to its
various contents. Under 'divisio legum' Melanchthon notes
'lex divina, lex naturae, leges humanae', and again under the
subdivision of the Mosaic law 'leges morales, ceremoniales et
forenses seu iudiciales' (21, 687). Which of these are valid for
the Christian? We find different answers at different stages in
Melanchthon's development: the first edition of the *Loci* (1521)
boldly proclaims that 'universa lex abrogata sit, non ceremoniae
tantum et iudiciorum formae, sed et decalogus, quod praestari
non potuit.... necesse est itaque fateri decalogum etiam anti-
quatum esse' (*CR*, 21, 198 sq., 194). The commentary on
Romans (1532), on the other hand, is quite definite in stating
that 'retinetur ergo decalogus, hoc est, lex illa communis omnium
hominum, quia et arguit peccata et docet spirituales cultus' (*CR*,
15, 722). A similar change, at least in emphasis, can be observed
in Luther (though it is, as shown by the dates of his utterances,
not simply the change from the 'young' to the 'old' Luther).
Dealing with the Apostles' decree (Acts xv, 28) in *Von den
Konziliis und Kirchen* (1539) he declares: 'This burden may be
interpreted to denote only the law of Moses and the circumcision,
not the ten commandments or good works. I am quite ready to
accept that; if thou canst keep the ten commandments more easily
than the ceremonies of Moses, go along and be more saintly
than St Peter and St Paul! I am so weak in the ten commandments that all ceremonies of Moses would seem to me much easier
to keep without the pressure of the ten commandments' (*WA*,
L, 562, 20 sq.). But disputing against the Antinomians in 1538,
he draws a very marked line between 'law' and 'circumcision'
and concludes: 'Isto vero sathanae discipuli videntur cogitare,

legem esse temporalem, quae sub Christo cessaverit, veluti est circumcisio' (*Disput.* Drews, p. 339, Th. 48). Thus both Luther and Melanchthon appear to reach the position held by the seventh of the Thirty-Nine Articles: 'Although the Law given from God by Moses, as touching Ceremonies and Rites, do not bind Christian men, nor the Civil precepts thereof ought of necessity to be received in any commonwealth: yet, notwithstanding, no Christian man whatsoever is free from the obedience of the Commandments which are called Moral.' Melanchthon's final argument to that effect is: 'The law does not last, because it is given by Moses, but because it is divinely written in the hearts. Itaque donec manet hominum natura, manet lex. The law of Moses does not concern us any more than the laws of Solon, therefore we are bound by the law not because of Moses but because it is written in nature' (*CR*, 12, 473). The ring is closed: the law must stand because God is God ('Deus non potest tolli') and man is man ('donec manet hominum natura'). Scriptural and natural theology unite against the Antinomian interpretation of the Gospel, and the concessions to the *lex naturae* open the door to, and result in, the very practical concessions to power.[1]

It is Melanchthon's special claim to have made room for the Law in the Church of the Gospel: 'Nequaquam esse Dei Ecclesiam eos coetus, qui contrariam doctrinam legi morali defendunt.... Comprehendo igitur in definitione Ecclesiae et legem moralem recte intellectam' (12, 367). And Luther readily pays him the tribute: 'Oh that we paid homage to M. Philippo who clearly and distinctly teaches about the function and use of the law' (*WA Ti*, 3, 3554); the whole fault of Agricola seems to him to be 'vult doctior esse quam Mag. Philippus et ego' (ibid. 4, 4912). Yet, easy as it was to defeat the 'anarchists' of the Reformation,[2] there were other heretical extremes to be avoided, and to make it clear beyond misunderstanding exactly how far the law is and is not an 'integral part' of the Gospel proved— as indeed it still proves to us—an extraordinarily difficult task. 'Christus aliquando ornat legem et servat, aliquando perrumpsit legem' (*WA Ti*, 4, 5172) is one of Luther's mildest words to describe the complexity of the question. In other places he had

---

[1] See below, Part IV and about this last connection in particular F. Hübner, *Natürliche Theologie und theokratische Schwärmerei bei Melanchthon*, Göttingen, 1936.

[2] 'Eos, qui contrariam doctrinam legi morali defendunt.'

said: 'summa igitur ars et sapientia Christianorum est nescire legem, ignorare opera et totam iustitiam activam' (*WA*, XL, 1, 43, 25).[1] Also Melanchthon is aware that there is no such thing as a *lex evangelica*: 'usitata *et falsa* distinctio est, tres esse leges, Naturalem, Mosaicam *et Evangelicam*' (*CR*, 12, 444); coordination of law and Gospel must never mean confusion. One is tempted to express the correlation in terms of the Chalcedonense. There is indeed an analogy between the two problems and an essential gain in knowing how *not* to conceive the unity of the two 'natures'. The position may become clearer when we consider it in this light and against the background of some interpretations with which Melanchthon was anxious *not* to be identified.

His first concern is for the via media between the 'Epicurean' view of the Antinomians and the Pharisaism of Rome: 'nec quid audacissime fingant Epicurei, qui sunt Antinomi, nec quid simulent monachi, qui iactitant se legi Dei obtemperare' (15, 886). The Formula Concordiae denounces the same error on the part of Schwenckfeldt: 'quod homo Christianus vere per Spiritum Dei renatus legem Dei in hac vita perfecte implere possit.'[2] Indeed, the 'rehabilitation' of the law must never be taken to indicate what in the case of Wesley has sometimes been described as his 'catholic retroversion'; there can be no 'synthesis' between the 'sola fide' and the decrees of Trent. Melanchthon's contemporaries were not altogether sure that 'Philippus' showed sufficient clarity and firmness in steering the right middle course between the two extremes of Major and Amsdorf;[3] and again the Formula Concordiae had not only to reject the two respective slogans 'bona opera necessaria esse ad salutem' and 'bona opera noxia esse ad salutem',[4] but found it also necessary to correct the latent synergistic tendency in Melanchthon's own position.[5] Nomism is a heresy as much as Antinomianism; Luther would hardly

[1] Melanchthon was hardly aware of the origin of this statement when he indignantly denounced it in the Articles of Worms: 'somebody has, in a public disputation at Nordhausen, made this proposition "summa ars Christianorum est nescire legem...". Whereas it is certainly the divine unchangeable truth to say: "Nova obedientia est necessaria"', *CR*, 9, 405.

[2] Cf. J. T. Müller's edition, p. 729, § v and above, p. 30, note 5.

[3] Cf. above, p. xvi, note.

[4] Cf. J. T. Müller's edition, p. 533, §§ i–ii.

[5] Cf. above, p. 22; W. Elert, *Morphologie des Luthertums*, München, 1931, I, 90. In the so-called Articles of Coswig, Melanchthon modifies his terms to meet the accusation 'that we had falsified the article on justification' and discourages the use of Major's phrase (*CR*, 9, 69). See below, pp. 79 sq.

have hesitated to call it the more dangerous of the two. In attributing to the good works the 'idiomata' of expiation and satisfaction—so he replies to his critics (*WA*, L, 597, 16 sq.)—they do not only rob Christ of what belongs to him alone but also spoil the very character and possibility of 'good' works. Melanchthon of course prefers to lay the emphasis on the positive and pedagogical aspect 'quod a tota lege liberati sumus, quod ad justificationem attinet, et tamen obedientiam incoari necesse est' (*CR*, 15, 723). In Geneva the note 'necesse est' is sounded with grim finality, and the danger of legalism is acute; not only is the 'balance' between St Paul and St James restored against Luther's 'one-sided' verdict on the latter, but the 'nova obedientia' of the Augustana turns definitely into the 'nova lex', and in the true succession of Calvin Karl Barth proceeds to proclaim that law is but the 'form', Gospel the 'matter' of scripture.

This is such an obvious departure from everything which has ever been said on the Lutheran side that it seems imperative to reconsider whether it was a wise move of Melanchthon to insist upon the 'tertius usus legis'[1] or whether this unhappy term does not rather mark the crucial turn beyond which the 'concessions to law' must not be carried. The intention is innocent enough when in exposition of 1 Tim. i, 9 ('Justo non est lex posita') he affirms against the 'anarchists' the 'triplex usus legis in renatis' 'quod ad obedientiam, quod ad doctrinam, quod ad reliquias peccati' (*CR*, 15, 1306 sq.), and when the Formula Concordiae repeats that according to St Paul (1 Cor. ix, 21) the Christian is 'not without law'.[2] Nor can it be denied that 'iusto *est* lex posita, quod ad vitam corporalem attinet, videlicet leges cibi, potus, politicae societatis' (*CR*, 15, 1016). But all this is logically implied in the 'primus usus' ('disciplinaris'). The dilemma in introducing the 'tertius usus' lies in the paradox that it can only apply to the 'reborn' inasmuch as he is 'not reborn'.[3] Melanchthon himself has to admit that 'when he ceases (!) to be just and violates, against his conscience, the commandments of God, then the Law again condemns him' (ibid.). What is characteristic of

---

[1] I.e. as 'guidance to the Church' (Vidler). The criticism here made was raised in Melanchthon's generation by Michael Neander (see O. Ritschl, *Dogmengeschichte des Protestantismus*, II, 418).

[2] J. T. Müller, op. cit. pp. 640, 643.

[3] The Chairman of a 'Religion and Life' meeting, attempting to create the broadest possible sympathies, is reported to have begun his address: 'Well, friends, I take it that we are, all of us here, reborn, more or less....'

the law is 'that it is called law when it is inwardly acknowledged as such, judging and accusing the hearts—not when the tables of the law hang on the walls' (15, 938); and that surely is *not* characteristic of the 'reborn'.[1] The Formula Concordiae makes that quite clear: 'quatenus renati sunt, ita quidem sponte ac libere, *quasi nullum praeceptum unquam accepissent...* '—so the law is fulfilled without the 'sting' of coaction. In other, and biblical, words, the old covenant is superseded by the new, and the fruits of the spirit, as the Formula Concordiae points out, take the place of the works of the law.[2] And that was precisely what Luther meant when he said: 'Where the law is, there is not the Holy Ghost' (*WA*, XVII, 125); it was what St Paul wrote to the Galatians: 'if ye be led of the Spirit, ye are not under the law' (v, 18). It is all-important that this 'aut-aut' should not become an 'et-et', that the original dualism in the Lutheran Law-Gospel-concept should be maintained: 'haec autem duo doctrinarum genera iam inde a condito mundo in ecclesia Dei, convenienti tamen discrimine, proposita fuere... quemadmodum D. Lutherus hoc discrimen in omnibus suis scriptis diligenter inculcavit, atque accurate monuit longe aliam Dei agnitionem ex evangelio quam ex lege hauriri.'[3] To have pressed this point was at any rate the *relative* right of Agricola's protest;[4] to digest it in a genuine and orthodox doctrine 'de gratia spiritus sancti applicatrice' is the still unfinished task of Lutheran theology.

On the other hand, there are signs that Melanchthon recognized the relativity of the pedagogical aspect which had moved him to use milk instead of strong meat. He is on safe Pauline ground when he explains that 'the doctrine of liberty is not understood by those who are not yet converted but wild and ungodly, unperturbed by the law of God' (*CR*, 14, 830; cf. 23, 83). The emergency which we found at the bottom of his rationing measures in the 'doctrina libertatis'[5] is the emergency not only of certain historical conditions, but of the human life as such: 'quia haec vita humana non potest carere certis ordinationibus, ut constat.'[6] Only in eschatology can the dualism of Law and Gospel be finally resolved.

[1] 'Justo non est lex posita, scilicet ad coactionem, item quo ad condemnationem', *CR*, 15, 1305.

[2] J. T. Müller, op. cit. p. 537, §§ IV–V.

[3] Formula Concordiae, op. cit. p. 638, §§ 22–23.

[4] See above, p. 36. [5] See above, p. 34.

[6] *CR*, 15, 724; cf. O. Ritschl, op. cit. II, 274, note 6.

B. THE FORENSIC ASPECT

The same impression of an unfinished task, the same necessity of an eschatological conclusion, will make itself felt when we turn to consider the transition from justification to sanctification in its 'purely' theological context as distinct from the previous chapter. It is evident throughout Melanchthon's writings that to him the new life of the believer forms a separate problem which is not settled by the formula 'sola fide'. The table-talks (*WA Ti*, 6, 6727) record one of his most illuminating conversations with Luther in which he repeatedly presses the question whether we are accounted righteous before God solely because of His mercy and the merit of Christ, or also, at least partly, because of the renovation wrought in us by the Holy Spirit. Luther firmly rejects any suggestion of dividing the work of the justifying grace into different parts—there is no 'stücklichte Ursach' (partial cause)[1]—and Melanchthon will later on make the utmost use of this argument against Augustine, Brenz and Osiander;[2] and yet, though they are in obvious agreement about the answer and Melanchthon only poses as *advocatus diaboli*, it is of more than rhetorical significance that it is he who must ask the question. To Luther it had never been doubtful that 'faith is always and incessantly in action, or else it is not faith. For what the works are or count, that they are or achieve through the glory and power of faith, which is the indispensable sun to their radiance';[3] he had never been able to understand how people—be they even St James!—could conceive of 'faith' without 'works'.[4] Melanchthon found it necessary to make sure of that by introducing his special 'concessions to law'; and having thus insisted on the 'tertius usus legis', he hastened to add: 'etiam post conversionem statuendum esse, iustam esse personam, id est, acceptam Deo ad vitam aeternam, propter Mediatorem, sola fide, per misericordiam,

---

[1] Cf. the *Anathema* in Formula Concordiae, op. cit. p. 530, § 21: 'IX. Credentes in Christum coram Deo iustos esse et salvos *simul* per imputatam Christi iustitiam *et* per inchoatam novam obedientiam, vel *partim* quidem per imputationem iustitiae Christi, *partim* vero per inchoatam novam obedientiam.'

[2] See above, p. xvi, note.

[3] *WA Ti*, 6, 6727: p. 151, 39 sq.; cf. p. 150, 33 sq.

[4] Ibid. p. 153, 4 sq.: 'This (sc. the necessity of works) is said against the feigned faith and sun; of the true faith and sun it would be ridiculous to speak like this!'

non propter propriam dignitatem virtutum, qualitatum, aut operum, etc.'[1] In his zeal for the good works he had gone so far as to provoke the suspicion, that 'they had falsified the article on justification';[2] therefore he had to exercise the greatest possible care in using the phrase 'propter fidem' lest faith itself in his conception should be mistaken for a 'work'. From the Apologia onwards the term 'iustum effici' is reduced to the meaning of 'iustum pronuntiari'; justification is the acquittal of the sinner, and the sentence 'simul justus, simul peccator' is strictly synthetical.[3] In order to take from the good works the weight of the divine 'idiomata' (see above, p. 42), the 'place' of our righteousness must be fixed 'in foro coeli'. The first move had been to 'complete' the 'sola fide'; the second is to restrict it; both are complementary in their motives; the pedagogical aspect leads to, and is balanced by, the forensic.

So we are faced with a new 'concession to law' on another level: no longer the 'addition' of the law to the Gospel, but the introduction of legal categories into the concept of the saving faith and the wording of the Gospel's good news in judicial terms. When, consequently, Hollaz, the last great dogmatic of the orthodoxy, writes, 'quae actio, cum sit extra hominem in Deo, non potest hominem intrinsece mutare', the critics would quote his very words to express their chief objection to Melanchthon: was not that just this, to rend asunder what God had joined together? Was not this the fatal corruption of Lutheranism, to make 'righteousness' in the literal sense 'of no effect'? Was not this to open the door to all the diseases of 'dialectical theology' and to provoke the Buchmanite reaction?

It would seem, then, that Melanchthon, so far from incorporating the 'new life' into his doctrine of salvation, succeeded only in narrowing the meaning of the 'sola fide' and removing the act of justification to the transcendental sphere. He appears to have forgotten 'that he which hath begun a good work in you will perform it until the day of Jesus Christ'; to have omitted what Holl pointed out to be the one, and the more important, half of Luther's organic and comprehensive view. The correction came from Osiander who claimed to restore the original Lutheran concept; and the issue was brought to a decision in the controversy

[1] CR, 15, 805–6, 1246; 14, 803; cf. 7, 783; 8, 890.
[2] See above, p. 41, note 5.
[3] See the controversy Holl-Walther, *Neue kirchliche Zeitschrift*, 1923–4.

on 'imputed' and 'essential' righteousness.[1] The tone of Osiander's polemics left little doubt as to his feelings about the fatal role played by Melanchthon: 'Ego credo, Philippum cum omnibus adhaerentibus ipsi esse mera mancipia Satanae... tanto artificio retinet speciem suae doctrinae, abnegata omni veritate eius, ut non credam pestilentiorem hominem in Ecclesia extitisse iam inde a temporibus apostolorum' (CR, 7, 726). His own aim is to forge the missing link between the second and third articles of the Creed; to proceed from the 'Christus pro nobis' to the 'Christus in nobis'; to interpret the text 'The Lord our righteousness' in what to-day would be called an 'incarnational' (rather than transcendental), 'sacramental' (rather than legal), 'Johannine' (rather than Pauline) way. His charge against Melanchthon's forensic aspect is that it produces a nomist view of God, a carnal view of man, and no view of the Holy Spirit. He could support his case with many passages from Luther such as this: 'Christ is God's grace, mercy, righteousness, truth, wisdom, power, comfort and salvation, given unto us without all merit. Christ, I say, not causaliter (as some people blindly put it), *as if he gave righteousness and remained outside*, for that is dead and never really given, unless Christ be there also Himself; like as the radiance of the sun and the heat of the fire is not, where there is no sun and fire.'[2]

Before we test this appeal to Luther and hear Melanchthon's reply, it will again be useful to draw the line from Osiander to Wesley; for it is precisely the same criticism which the founder of Methodism offers to the Moravian doctrine of 'imputed righteousness' and which colours his general verdict on Lutheranism. Nor is the tone of it any less certain than was Osiander's: in a hymn 'for those that are turned out of the Way' Wesley prays for the conversion of the 'happy sinners' on the Moravian side:

> O wouldst thou break the fatal snare,
> Of carnal self-security,
> And let them *feel* the wrath they bear,
> And let them groan their want of Thee,
> Robb'd of their false pernicious peace,
> Their *self* (*imputed*) righteousness!

[1] See O. Ritschl, *Dogmengeschichte des Protestantismus*; E. Hirsch, *Die Theologie des Andreas Osiander*, Göttingen, 1919; Salig, *Historie der Augsburgischen Confession*, II, 951–9.

[2] *WA*, I, 219, 30 sq.; note the exact correspondence of the metaphor to that quoted on p. 44 on the relation between faith and works.

> The men of careless lives, who deem
> Thy righteousness *accounted* theirs,
> Awake out of the soothing dream,
> Alarm their souls with humble fears,
> Thou jealous God, stir up thy power,
> And let them sleep in sin no more.

More pleasing sounds the application to his own state of piety:

> Thy righteousness is counted mine;
> When will it in my nature shine?

And

> I cannot rest in sins forgiven;
> Where is the earnest of its heaven?[1]

Here, in the last passage, is the clearest indication of a decisive step *beyond* Luther which Wesley feels bound to take. Too great is the urge of the 'revival' to be content with the Pauline 'wait for the hope of righteousness by faith'; the goal is *perfection* 'here below', and it must be reached by what Wesley himself significantly calls a 'short cut':

> Finish thy great work of love,
> *Cut it short* in righteousness,
> Fit me for the realms above,
> Change, and bid me die in peace.[2]

To Zinzendorf's argument that 'a believer is never sanctified or holy in himself, but in Christ only', he replies: 'Does a believer love God, or does he not? If he does, he has the love of God in him. Is he lowly, or meek, or patient at all? If he is, he has these tempers in himself.... You cannot therefore deny, that every believer has holiness in, though not from, himself; else you deny that he is holy at all; and if so, he cannot see the Lord.'[3] Scripture seems to provide strong evidence for this; the first Johannine epistle speaks continuously about the believer having the truth, or seed, or life of God *in* him (cf. i, 8, 10; iii, 9, 15, etc.). But Wesley only needed to refer to his favourite verse Phil. ii, 5:

[1] The hymn 'For those that are turned out of the Way' is printed in full in the second edition of *A short view of the difference between the Moravian Brethren, lately in England, and the Rev. Mr John and Charles Wesley*, Bristol, 1748. The other two quotations are from *Short hymns on passages select from Holy Scripture*, 1762, and from the present *Methodist Hymn Book*, No. 280.

[2] From the 1874 *Methodist Hymn Book*, No. 287, verse 6; 402, verse 2; etc.

[3] *Works*, x, 203.

'let this mind be in you which was also in Christ Jesus.' On the other hand, he finds it extremely difficult to trace the term 'imputed righteousness' back to a scriptural basis.[1] This fact in itself does not prejudice him—'we do no more deny the phrase than the thing'—but it makes him very tolerant as to the use of the expression 'we are unwilling to obtrude it on other men' (*Works*, v, 243). Twice he quotes a sentence from Hervey: 'We are not solicitous as to any particular set of phrases. Only let men be humbled as repenting criminals at Christ's feet, let them rely as devoted pensioners on his merits, and they are undoubtedly in the way to a blessed immortality.'[2] The whole sermon on 'The Lord our righteousness' is remarkable for its emphasis upon the relativity of theological language; we shall have to come back to this.[3] What concerns us here directly is the final twofold warning against the fanatics who either ridicule or standardize the term; to Robert Barclay 'who scruples not to say: Imputed righteousness—imputed nonsense!'[4] he answers: 'And why should you be angry at an expression? "O, it has been abused!" And what expression has not?'[5]; to the others, who 'represent me as a Papist' and 'make tragical outcries, as though I were subverting the very foundations of Christianity', he says: 'Allow me the right of private judgment...and be not angry with me if I cannot judge it proper to use any one expression every two minutes.'[5] In defence of 'imputed righteousness' he takes great pains to prove from his various writings that since 1738 he has never wavered from the Reformation doctrine of justification;[6] and he goes a long way to meet Melanchthon when he confines his belief in 'inherent righteousness' to 'its proper place; not as the ground of our acceptance with God; but as the fruit of it; not in the place of imputed righteousness, but as consequent upon it',[7] and when he is careful not to let 'faith' become a 'work' which could take the place of Christ: 'God gives this faith; in that moment we are accepted of God; and yet, not for the sake of that faith, but of what Christ has done and suffered

---

[1] *Works*, x, 315; ix, 397.
[2] Ibid. and x, 315. Cf. Heinrich Vogel's statement in *Acht Artikel evangelischer Lehre* (which I must quote from memory here): 'wir sind nicht Rentner, die von ihrem religiösen Kapital, sondern Bettler, die im Glauben leben.'
[3] See below, Chapter v.
[4] Wesley, *Works*, v, 243.
[5] Ibid. p. 245.
[6] Ibid. pp. 239 sq.
[7] Ibid. p. 241.

for us.'[1] Zinzendorf's 'Jesu, thy blood and righteousness' is not only not banished from the Wesleyan hymn books, but quoted with special favour over and over again! If that was consistent with Wesley's polemic against the Moravians ('who are the most plausible, and therefore far the most dangerous, of all the Antinomians now in England'),[2] then it is less surprising to find him in sympathy both with Osiander and Melanchthon; and then his heretical tendency towards perfectionism is but the counter-offensive to the extreme quietism of the other side.

Indeed, Melanchthon himself knows of that aspect 'on which there is no dispute between us'[3] and admits: 'there also must be urged in the Churches the doctrine of God's indwelling and working in the faithful and reconciled; for renovation must follow.'[4] The question is again (as in the last chapter) about the order and place of the 'novitas vitae' within the 'corpus doctrinae'. 'At nostrae Ecclesiae concedunt, oportere in nobis esse novitatem...sed propter hanc novitatem non habet homo remissionem peccatorum et reconciliationem. Sed prius accipienda est remissio et reconciliatio (quae sunt iustificatio propter mediatorem Deum et hominem) fide.'[5] This 'Scriptum de Osiandro' comprises three fundamental charges of heresy. First, in ascribing man's justification to the indwelling Spirit, Osiander proves himself a 'papist'; it is only a difference of emphasis when he dwells on the cause, and the Scholastics on the effects, of that divine inhabitation; in either case the centre of salvation is shifted from the throne of the heavenly grace to the 'qualitas infusa'. Secondly, in neglecting the distinction between the work of Christ on the cross and the fruits of the spirit in us—'prius accipienda est remissio'—Osiander confuses the trinitarian faith and degrades the final 'propter Christum' into a merely preparatory 'per' (CR, 8, 557, 559). Thirdly, in abandoning the obedience of Christ as the proper cause of our redemption, Osiander becomes guilty of isolating the person from the work and the Godhead from the manhood;[6] the Formula Concordiae seals his condemnation as it lists and rejects the errors: 'Christum esse iustitiam

---

[1] Ibid. p. 242.   [2] Ibid. x, 201.

[3] Sc. himself and Osiander; CR, 7, 892 sq., 895.

[4] CR, 8, 576.   [5] CR, 7, 783.

[6] 'Propter mediatorem Deum et hominem', ibid. xxx. On the distinctions between divine and human, external and internal, active and passive righteousness see also Wesley's sermon on Jer. xxiii, 6 in Works, v, 236 sq.

nostram solummodo secundum divinam naturam....Christum esse iustitiam nostram tantummodo iuxtam humanam naturam.'[1] The supporting biblical arguments are taken from Gal. v, 5,[2] from John xvi, 10,[3] from Rom. vi, 23,[4] and from Dan. ix, 18.[5] All these points are summed up in the definition of the 'iustitia Christi': 'Intelligitur ergo primum iustitia Christi, ipsius obedientia qua nos vestit et tegit. Christus est nobis iustitia, id est, ipsius obedientia est illa res, propter quam habemus reconciliationem et acceptationem in hac vita' (CR, 23, 517). What is the theological motive behind this insistence upon the 'Christus extra nos'? It is, as in all Melanchthon's writings and particularly in the Apologia, to safeguard the glory of Christ and the peace of the soul.[6] Only in the transcendental act of its acquittal 'in foro coeli' can man's tormented conscience come to rest; and as the word from heaven declares and pronounces to his people, being penitent, the absolution and remission of their sins, so the sacrament gives to them the same objective assurance of the gracious God by the very externity of the real presence.[7] Melanchthon has no doubt that this is the one, only and eternal truth of the Gospel, witnessed by the patriarchs, prophets, apostles, oecumenical symbols, 'and in these latter days again revealed by D. Martinus Luther' (CR, 8, 579); in contrast to which Osiander 'takes away the consolation of the imputata justitia...and diverts our trust from the obedience of Christ towards the renovation within ourselves' (CR, 9, 403).

But, strangely enough, it is the same theological motives which guide Osiander in his reply when he observes that 'imputata

[1] Op. cit. p. 529, §§ 12–13.

[2] 'Although it is true that God dwells in the conversion and that the life eternal, wrought by Christ the Lord, must begin in this life, yet there is a difference between the saints in the resurrection and the saints in this life', CR, 7, 895.

[3] 'That he himself shall be our righteousness before God imputative, as Christ himself says: haec est iustitia vestra, quod ego ad patrem vado', CR, 8, 574.

[4] 'That eternal life is a gift, given to us by grace for Christ's sake', CR, 8, 578.

[5] 'Not for our righteousnesses, but for thy great mercies', CR, 8, 559.

[6] 'Hos (sc. pavores conscientiae) si considerarent, scirent mentes perterrefactos quaerere consolationem extra sese, et hanc consolationem esse fiduciam, qua voluntas acquiescit in promissione misericordiae propter mediatorem donatae', CR, 21, 743. S. Elert, op. cit. I, 91.

[7] Cf. Gollwitzer, 'Luthers Abendmahlslehre', in Abendmahlsgemeinschaft?, München, 1937, p. 118.

iustitia est frigidior glacie' (ibid.) and suspects that Melanchthon's doctrine will produce 'secure' people (7, 898 sq.). He is as much concerned as his adversaries about the 'totus Christus', and to him the forensic aspect of the redemption is evidence of a defective Christology. One of Melanchthon's friends shows himself obviously impressed by the Osiandric thought 'ut, quum haberemus non tantum imputativam ab Adamo et labem et damnationem, quomodo non in Christo etiam praeter imputativam habeamus talem iustitiam inhaerentem et personalem ad vitam, qualem ad mortem' (7, 309). A similar deduction could be made from the description of Judas in Psalm cix, 18: 'as he clothed himself with cursing, like as with his garment, so let it come into his bowels like water, and like oil into his bones'; should not the same 'effect' be attributed to the 'robe of righteousness' (Job xxix, 14; Psalm cxxxii, 9, 16; Is. lxi, 10)? And does not the Formula Concordiae point in the same direction when it emphatically denies 'quod non Deus ipse, sed dona Dei duntaxat in credentibus habitent' and that true faith 'existere et manere possit in eiusmodi homine, qui non vere poenitentiam habeat, et qui caritate sit vacuus et in peccatis contra conscientiam perseveret'?[1]

There is sufficient material to justify the suggestion[2] that Osiander, whatever his faults, had at least seen 'the other side' of Luther which Melanchthon was apt to forget; and among the Reformers Brenz[3] firmly held that the 'forensic' and the 'dynamic' aspects of justification were not really incompatible. To him the controversy appeared to be a mere *bellum grammaticale*;[4] he was able to appeal to Osiander 'per illam divinam iusticiam, quam tu urges et qua nos speramus perpetuo fruituros'[5] and to silence Melanchthon at Worms in 1557.[6] His considered opinion is: 'Scimus divina clementia unam esse certam, constantem, veram et perpetuam sententiam coelestis doctrinae. Sed quaerimus hic, quemadmodum antea commemoravi, quam recte, quam apte vel

---

[1] Op. cit. p. 624, §§ 64–5.
[2] Made by E. Hirsch, *Die Theologie des Andreas Osiander*, Göttingen, 1919.
[3] See above, p. xvi, note.
[4] See Pressel, *Anecdota Brentiana*, Tübingen, 1868, p. 356.
[5] Ibid. p. 337.
[6] See the report of a contemporary: 'to Osiandrism he made no reference but passed it over in silence because Brentius and the theologians from Wuerttemberg were present who are altogether Osiandrists and do not want to condemn him in any way', *CR*, 9, 270; cf. 273; similarly 7, 726.

illorum vel Osiandri dogma cum hac una certa et coelesti doctrina ac veritate conveniat.'[1]

Luther himself, in a postscript to a letter from Melanchthon to Brenz, remarks: 'I am used to thinking as if there was within my heart no quality or virtue, which could be called faith or charity, but I trust entirely in Christ and say: My formalis iustitia, that is, my certain, abiding, perfect righteousness wherein nothing is lacking, but which is as it ought to be before God—that is Christ, my Lord', and goes on to refute the mere moral and didactic interpretation of Christ by quoting John xiv, 6 and 2 Cor. v, 21: 'He does not say: I point or give to you the way, the truth and the life, as if He worked this in me while being elsewhere outside me; no, in me He shall abide, live and speak...' (*WA Ti*, 3, 3131). Osiander would have gladly signed this; still more would he have been in sympathy with Luther's favourite parable of the 'exchange' between the bridegroom's righteousness and the bride's sin,[2] and with the famous description of faith as 'a divine work within us which changes and regenerates us from God, mortifying the old Adam, making us quite new men in heart, mind and all powers and bringing the Holy Spirit with it', which concludes: 'Righteousness is such faith and is called God's righteousness or that which counts before Him.'[3] The keynote here, and in so many parallel passages, which naturally must appeal to Osiander is 'vita experimentalis' (*WA*, 11, 499, 20 sq.), the exact counterpart to the 'forensic aspect'. Yet all this is not Luther's final word. Wherever he deals with 'experience' he sounds paradoxical: preaching on the witness of the Spirit within us (Rom. viii, 16) he declares: 'this witness is such that we also feel and sense the power of the Holy Spirit which is wrought in us by His Word, and that our experience tallies with the Word of preaching' (*WA*, XXII, 139, 1 sq.); and yet with equal emphasis he insists: 'Where thou must believe, thou must not cling to what thy thinking or feeling telleth thee, but what the Word of God telleth thee, however little thou feelest it' (ibid. 338, 12 sq.). A sentence fundamental for his whole theology is 'certe magna est res sentire contra sensum suum' (*WA*, XXXII, 26, 1). How can the two statements be reconciled? In an early exposition of the fifth petition in the Lord's Prayer we find an answer which

[1] Pressel, op. cit. p. 360.
[2] In 'De libertate Christiana', *WA*, VII, 25, 26 sqq.
[3] Preface to Romans, *WA*, Deutsche Bibel, VII, 10, 6 sq., 28 sq.

is as fascinating as it is profound: 'This prayer may be interpreted in two ways. First, that God forgives our trespasses secretly and without our feeling, like as He retains the sins of many who neither feel them nor care. Secondly, publicly and with our feeling, like as He marks the iniquities of some so that they feel it through penalties and terrors of conscience. The first forgiveness is always necessary; the other sometimes in order that man should not despair. ...The first is by faith only and achieves much, the other by feeling and has its reward. The first is used with the strong in faith, the other with the weak and beginners' (*WA*, ii, 116, 27 sq.; 117, 15 sq.). The distinction is not simply that between Melanchthon and Osiander,[1] but it helps to explain why the generation after Luther could only grasp the parts of what he held together. It also shows the balance between the witness of the Spirit and the echo of our own spirit which Wesley in his Standard Sermons was anxious to restore.[2] In the same direction points the last of Luther's 'anti-forensic' utterances which we must quote from his early commentary on the Psalter: 'Lex est verbum Dei ad nos, Evangelium autem verbum dei in nos. Aliud enim est in nos, aliud ad nos loqui. In nos enim efficax est et capit nos, ad nos autem nequaquam. Ita verbum fidei penetrat ut gladius anceps in interiora et spiritum sanctificat' (*WA*, iv, 9, 27 sq.).

Here both Osiander and Melanchthon are put in their place. Osiander is wrong in replacing 'in nos' by 'in nobis' and opening the door to 'enthusiast' conceptions of the 'inner word'. Melanchthon is wrong in restricting justification to a 'verbum ad nos'; the forensic aspect, correct in itself, misleads him to think of the Gospel in terms of the Law. In spite of numerous reassuring phrases[3]

[1] Holl's well-known criticism is based on Melanchthon's one-sided interest in the consolatory value of doctrine, cf. *CR*, 15, 1159: 'consolatio finis doctrinae.'

[2] 'Everyone must believe solely because it is God's Word and he feels inwardly that it is the truth', *WA*, x, 2, 90, 10 sq.; 'but thou must feel within thy own conscience Christ Himself and be absolutely sure that it is God's Word if even all the world would fight against it; as long as thou hast not that feeling as long thou hast certainly not yet tasted the Word of God', ibid. 23, 6 sq.

[3] *CR*, 14, 355: 'Non solum dat verbum Christus, ut caeteri Prophetae, sed ipse admovet manus, ut testetur se efficacem esse, et non ociosum.' 14, 1002: 'Tota nostra vita debet esse confessio' (ad Matt. v, 16). 15, 913: 'Fit igitur et in nobis mutatio, et quomodo fiat, in vera conversione, in doloribus et consolatione discimus.' 15, 631: 'Ultimus effectus (sc. gratiae) est consummatio totius naturae nostrae et novitas, et vita aeterna.' 15, 637: 'sepeliri cum Christo', etc.

he falls short of the biblical promise of the new covenant; which is 'not in tables of stone, but in fleshy tables of the heart'.[1] The danger is that the Word remains 'standing beside' us in its forensic purity while we continue in the *status quo*; that radical preaching (as in the case of Hoskyns) results in reactionary practice; that justification of sinners comes to mean justification of sin. This is what Osiander had in mind when he called the *iustitia imputativa* 'frigidior glacie'; in all his heresies he is aiming rightly at the penetration of the Word 'ut gladius anceps in interiora'. What precisely is the relevance, he asks, of the 'forum coeli' to the 'forum cordis'? What difference does it make in reality that Christ is our righteousness? The test of 'realism' can nowhere be more crucial than in the field of politics, and it is here that we must expect Melanchthon to reap what he has sown in his basic 'concessions to Law'.

[1] Cf. again Luther, *WA*, II, 499, 20: 'vitaque experimentalis, res quoque ipsa, quae scribitur digito solo Dei in cordibus.'

CHAPTER IV

CONCESSIONS TO POWER

A. STATE INTERESTS

The transition from the heavenly to the earthly 'status' of the Christian is made in Melanchthon's description of the victory of Christ: 'Haec victoria est initium conformitatis cum resurrectione Christi. Est autem haec victoria hoc ipsum in nobis, quod vocatur novitas Spiritus et non est tantum cogitatio humana... sed ipse Filius Dei est efficax per vocem Evangelii in cordibus credentium et facit eos suae resurrectioni conformes.... The Anabaptists when they hear these words, mortification and vivification, feign things which are quite different from penitence and conversion; then they pretend mortification to be simulated gestures of humility, contempt of political order and matrimony, common ownership of goods, etc.... Nos loquimur de rebus notis in Ecclesia, et in exerciciis piorum' (*CR*, 15, 927). It is most important to note that the polemics against the Anabaptists follow immediately upon the assertion of the 'Christus efficax' and form, in fact, the context within which the 'concessions to power' should be considered. Once again we see the Reformers on their guard against a fatal misunderstanding of the 'libertas Christiana': as Luther protested that it did surely not mean the peasants' plea for abolition of slavery,[1] so Melanchthon is careful to keep what he has to say about the newness of life 'in Ecclesia, et in exerciciis piorum'. Biblical examples serve to illustrate his forensic aspect of liberty: 'So David had liberty while on flight. So the three men at Babylon had liberty in the furnace, as the Son of God was manifestly with them. So Daniel had liberty among the lions.'[2] That Christ makes intercession for us at the right hand of God, is no warrant for us to take the kingdom by force; on the contrary, the Holy Spirit whom He sends down from heaven, 'visibili specie, ut in Apostolos, ita in Romanos milites (!) in magna frequentia concionis effusus est'.[3] He is on the side of the powers which He has ordained, and Melanchthon

---

[1] 'This is to make Christian liberty carnal altogether', *WA*, XVIII, 326, 33.
[2] *CR*, 14, 829; ad John viii, 36.
[3] *CR*, 11, 922; the context is Acts x.

can even speak of the 'praesentia Dei in conservatione ordinis politici' (*CR*, 11, 1012; 16, 422).

This course was dictated not only by historical necessity: the desire to avoid both hierarchy and anarchy in politics, though obviously accentuated by the warning examples of Rome on the one side and Anabaptist Münster on the other, was a sound theological motive. 'For the kingdom of God is not meat and drink; but righteousness, and peace, and joy in the Holy Ghost'— that was a clear scriptural denunciation of the two errors, and it spelt true spiritualism in doctrine (the forensic aspect) and true realism in politics (concessions to state interests). The adversaries were in constant danger of confusing that proportion, either by quietist retreat from, or by theocratic invasion of, the secular 'order'.[1] 'Quam stulte iudicent ii, qui somniant in Evangelio praecipi quandam Platonicam rerum communionem aut monasticam abdicationem proprietatis...atque hic exaggeranda est autoritas legum naturae et magistratuum...imo Evangelio contumeliam afficiunt, qui fingunt Evangelium novam quandam doctrinam esse de mutandis politicis rebus.'[2] Whereas the plain truth of the Word of God is: 'as little as architecture or music conflict with the Gospel, so politics have no quarrel with the Gospel' (21, 544). Every detail here is significant: the sneer at 'Platonism' in general and the rejection of 'communism' in particular which includes Wycliffe's ideas about property; the abhorrence of all revolutionary ways and means ('de mutandis politicis rebus'); the proclamation of true evangelical liberty against monastic legalism ('monasticam abdicationem') and the confident comparison of 'politia' with 'architectonica aut Musica'; the coordination of 'magistratus' with 'leges naturae'. In analysing these points we shall be able to trace Melanchthon's concessions to power back to their origin in the concessions to tradition, reason and law.

It is typical of Melanchthon that he dreads nothing so much as the charge of sedition; but in dissociating himself from the

---

[1] Cf. *CR*, 16, 419 sq. on the 'discrimen Evangelii et politices', and Elert, op. cit. II, 278, 351, etc.

[2] *CR*, 21, 462; cf. 11, 68. In another passage (*CR*, 9, 1003) Melanchthon distinguishes between the 'seditious errors' and the 'dogmatic blasphemies' of the Anabaptists and suggests 'primum recte docendi sunt' as the first stage of treatment in either case; failing this, 'si sunt pertinaces', they are to be punished according to the principle: 'Dei potestati resistent, poenam sibi acquirent' (cf. Matt. xxvi, 52).

'tumultuous' forerunners and partisans of the Reformation,[1] he can count upon the company not only of Luther, but also of St Paul. 'Neither against the law of the Jews, nor against the temple, nor against Caesar, have I offended at all' (Acts xxv, 8) is an emphasis common to the New Testament (in particular see the trials in Acts and the Passion narrative) and the Lutheran tradition. There is an obvious tendency towards 'retinendam tranquillitatem et augendam reverentiam erga magistratum' and a strong suspicion that all those anarchists on the other side 'cum doceant Evangelium, irrumpant in alienam doctrinam' (CR, 16, 419); the difficulty, to us, seems to be that such words are apt to represent the desire of the old Adam as much as the demand of the Christian conscience. 'The Church must have nothing to do with politics—except conservative politics!' Indeed, Melanchthon pronounces unhesitatingly in favour of the status quo: 'praesentem statum retinendum esse ac mutari non posse' (16, 429); and once again the common sense of Aristotle is given preference before the vision of Plato.[2] That there is another aspect both in Luther and the New Testament, that the Gospel, while producing the 'best citizens', is also essentially the source of 'rebellion', that the same book of Acts (xvi, 20; xvii, 6) contains the charge, not wholly unjust, 'these men have turned the world upside down... they exceedingly trouble our city'—appears to have been forgotten or passed by in silence.

Yet, in one sense, the Anabaptists are reactionaries and Melanchthon the champion of progress. While they adhere to the strict and literal use of the Mosaic law even in the courts,[3] to him the very fact of the destruction of the 'politia Mosaica' in history is evidence that in God's will it was not meant to survive.[4] So he insists upon the variability of the laws according to time and place and argues: 'sicut autem Christianus alias alio vestitu utitur, seu ut alibi aliis dierum spatiis utitur: ita licet ei uti cuiuscunque loci politia' (CR, 16, 419; cf. 21, 984). As the parable of the garment shows, he has the Gospel solidly behind him, and again, he is equally sure of St Paul's Placet when he ranks the 'regimen

---

[1] 'Wicleff valde tumultuatur', 16, 419.

[2] 'Platonis vero politia prorsus a natura abhorret...', CR, 16, 429.

[3] 'Damnabat omnes leges ab Ethnicis conditas; contendebat in foro Jus ex Mose discendum esse, non intelligens vim et naturam Christianae libertatis', CR, 2, 31; cf. CR, 21, 198–205.

[4] 'Deus ostenderet non oportere perpetuam esse, funditus et horribili exemplo delevit', CR, 21, 1007; cf. 687.

corporale' alongside with meat and drink among the things
'which God hath created to be received with thanksgiving'; all
this falls under the heading of 'exteriores res', the use of which
is not the subject of scriptural ruling, but of Christian freedom
(21, 227 sq.; 16, 449 etc.).[1] Thus the Magna Charta of Article
XVI in the *Conf. Aug.* (cf. Art. 37 of the 39): 'de rebus civilibus
docent, quod legitimae ordinationes civiles sint bona opera Dei,
quod Christianis liceat...' includes the offices of 'gerere magistratus' (*CR*, 11, 912; 23, 85 sq.), 'exercere iudicia' (11, 68 sq.;
12, 699), 'iure bellare' (21, 227 sq.), 'tenere proprium' (16,
549 sq.), 'iusiurandum postulantibus magistratibus dare' (16,
453 sq.); and it marks the final break with all 'enthusiasts' by
the corresponding Anathema: 'Damnant et illos, qui evangelicam
perfectionem non collocant in timore Dei et fide, sed in deserendis
civilibus officiis, quia evangelium tradit iusticiam aeternam cordis.'
Only in the first edition of the *Loci* (*CR*, 21, 200) we find
the reservation: 'contendere iudicio Christianis non licet'—a
surprising recollection of 1 Cor. vi. Otherwise the line of
defence remains unbroken: 'all things are lawful for me.'
Did Melanchthon, we wonder, ever pause to consider the
following sentence in that context: 'but all things are not
expedient' (1. Cor. x, 23)?

He did, indeed, make ample allowance for that in the field of
ecclesiastical diplomacy (see the next chapter), but we are now
concerned with secular politics. And here, surely, the general
motto 'Christiano licet' cannot be sufficient; the 'iusticia aeterna
cordis' cannot mean that the Gospel is simply indifferent to the
course and direction of the 'res exteriores'. Melanchthon's
'themata de duplici iustitia' (*CR*, 21, 227 ff.), although drawn
up for the purpose of discrimination, imply of necessity some
kind of positive relation between divine (spiritual) and human
(corporal) righteousness, or, in terms of Romans, the absolute 'we
have peace with God through our Lord Jesus Christ' (v, 1) and the
relative 'if it be possible, as much as lieth in you, live peaceably with
all men' (xii, 18) or, again, in terms of Luther, 'that a little righteousness might be on earth; for the righteousness of God is out of
the question here' (*WA*, 20, 355, 32). The dangerous categorical
statement 'quod Evangelium ad cordis iustitiam pertinet, non
pertinet ad civilem statum' (!) is therefore supplemented by the
condition 'imo approbat omnes formas rerum publicarum, modo

[1] See above, p. 39.

sint consentaneae rationi'.[1] While there is no such thing as 'evangelical politics', there is the vital distinction between 'politia recta et corrupta' (16, 436); and the freedom of the Christian in political decision and action must never be 'an occasion to the flesh': 'non sunt alligati Christiani ad ullius gentis politiam; sed possunt uti imperiis et legibus politicis, *non pugnantibus cum naturali ratione*, ubicunque vivunt' (23, 82; cf. 14, 829; 15, 722). Reason and the law of nature are the criteria by which all particular human codes are to be judged; in so far as they pass that test, it is safe to assume that they belong to the 'traditionibus, in quibus nihil contra scripturam decretum est' (21, 227 f.). It is Melanchthon's conviction that among the systems of legislature the *ius Romanum* is still the best to answer this description,[2] and that to the *ius Romanum* is ultimately due what measure of 'humanity' we have preserved so far (cf. 11, 361). The magistrates are right in basing jurisdiction on this source; there is no objection or alternative to it offered in Holy Writ: 'et cum hae res subiectae sint rationi, nihil opus est in scriptura singulas artes tradere' (16, 449).

Thus once again we find Melanchthon in the school of Rome and easily recognize the link with what has been said earlier about the concessions to tradition and reason in his theology. The substitution in politics of a Gentile authority for the Mosaic one and the general identification of the decalogue with the *lex naturae*[3] is the clearest objective expression of his innate anti-fanatical, anti-enthusiast, anti-revolutionary bias. But it does not only separate him for ever from the 'Schwärmer'; it also carries him to a certain extent beyond Luther. In contrast to his master, he has little use for German law as compared with Roman;[4] and in the centre of his political thought stands the Latin idea of 'societas' which is 'naturrechtlich' to the core and alien to the mentality, if not to the vocabulary, of Luther.[5] It is inevitable,

[1] *CR*, 16, 419; note again the parallel 'sicut approbat architectonicam, aut medicinam rationi consentaneam'.

[2] '...quae de omnibus civilibus officiis, de judiciis, de contractibus ita praecipiunt, ut nusquam a natura, nusquam a ratione discedere intelligantur', *CR*, 16, 446.

[3] See Elert, op. cit. pp. 346 ff.

[4] 'Nam hoc Jus Romanum haud dubie erudita Philosophia est....Nec vero mihi legenti vetera ac barbarica iura horridae gentis Germanicae, ut sunt Westvalici ritus, venit in mentem perinde hanc nationem factam cultiorem acceptis Romanis legibus...', 11, 353.

[5] Cf. Elert, op. cit. 11, 344; Elert, 'Societas bei Melanchthon', in *Festschrift für L. Ihmels*, 1928.

and in fact most desirable for Melanchthon, that this trend should
provide a link with the Church of Rome; the *Augustana* is
notorious for its tendency towards 'appeasement' (in the same
degree as it is hostile towards the 'left wing' of the Reformation);
and to-day we have come to rediscover the significance of the
'lex naturae' as the only possible common ground for cooperation between the two Churches in the field of 'life and work'.[1]
Here Melanchthon's 'concessions to Politics' take a further
crucial turn; 'natural theology' leads directly to 'theocracy'.[2]
This will become clear when we examine his conception of the
magistrate.

The starting point is, as for Luther, the insistence—against
the Anabaptists—upon the difference between 'latrocinium' and
'magistratus' (*CR*, 16, 247) and the restoration—after the papal
distortions—of the 'dignitas rerum politicarum' (21, 542 ff.,
984 ff.). Both anarchists and hierarchists violate the divine right
of the state order. God does not condemn empires as such because
of the injustices existent in their midst (cf. 23, 87); and the tyrannic
abuse of power does not invalidate the proper parental exercise
of princely functions. Magistrates, as well as teachers, have their
appointed place with the parents in the fifth (Luther: fourth)
commandment: 'parentum loco sunt' (21, 227). Their duty is
to keep order and to restrain, where necessary, the criminal by
force; they can authorize the lawful use of the sword in the hands
of hangman and warrior;[3] and it can be shown from scriptural
examples where kings or judges have overstepped their competence (cf. 21, 227 ff.). Patriarch and policeman jointly form the
pattern for the Lutheran type of 'magistrate'—'for the punishment of evildoers and for the praise of them that do well'; the
state must needs be regarded as minister both of wrath and of
grace.[4] No doubt it is in accordance with Rom. xiii, that favourite
passage of the Reformers, when Luther says: 'Magistratus poli-
ticus est signum gratiae divinae, quod Deus sit misericors'
(*WA Ti*, 1, No. 162), and when Melanchthon attests 'magistratus
et politicas ordinationes non sic a Deo esse sicut permitti mala

[1] See the Encyclicals and documents connected with the German Church
Conflict and the 'Sword of the Spirit' Movement in England.
[2] See F. Hübner, op. cit.
[3] 'Si fieri nequit ut prorsus nemo laedatur, ut agatur, ut paucissimi
laedantur, sublatis iis qui publicam quietem interturbant, et in hoc magistratus
poenaque sontibus constituantur', *CR*, 21, 119.
[4] See Elert, op. cit. II, 336, 293 ff.

dicuntur, sed docent positive res esse, quas Deus aliquo suo opere efficaciter et instituit et conservat et verbo approbat' (*CR*, 21, 546).

All this is not really controversial if the presupposition is sound that the Gospel does allow and contain 'concessions to politics' at all. The problem arises when Melanchthon goes beyond the boundaries of Rom. xiii, begins to 'fill in' what the New Testament left open, and tries in particular to define the relationship of State and Church. We have already noted his reference to the 'praesentia Dei in ordine politico' (see above, p. 56); he proceeds to trace the 'numinosum' in the establishment and maintenance of the 'societas'[1] and to expound, as Luther had done before him, Psalm lxxxii: 'ye are gods' (cf. 16, 91). He rejects the theory of a mere *Polizeistaat* which loses sight of the higher purpose of 'magistrates';[2] that higher purpose is the knowledge and worship of God which is the goal of all human life[3] and which also the State is destined to serve. With this 'finis societatis' in view the magistrate must properly be described as 'custos societatis humanae';[4] and special stress is laid on the point that 'magistratus est custos primae et secundae tabulae legis, quod ad externam disciplinam attinet' (16, 87). As the secular authorities are not only 'in loco parentum', but, like the parents themselves, 'in loco Dei', obedience to the fifth commandment is indeed part of the 'first table' no less than of the second.

Had it seemed then, a moment ago, that the Gospel is not concerned with politics, we learn now very definitely that politics are concerned with the Gospel. 'Ostendi pertinere emendationem Ecclesiarum ad magistratus officium...valde errant principes, si hanc curam non pertinere ad se arbitrantur' (21, 1012 ff.). These words call upon the head of the State as 'praecipuum membrum Ecclesiae'[5] to lend his arm to the Church—even to the end of 'emendatio. Ecclesiarum'!—and they prepare the way for the formation of the ominous *landesherrliche Kirchenregiment*.

[1] 'Nec posset humana ope tantum retineri, sed experientia testatur aliquo numine ad poenam rapi eos, qui violant hunc ordinem', *CR*, 21, 642.

[2] 'Errant igitur magistratus, qui divellunt gubernationem a fine, et se tantum pacis ac ventris custodes esse existimant', ibid.

[3] See the Genevan Catechism.

[4] *CR*, 21, 1011: 'Aristoteles erudite tradidit definitionem magistratus paucissimis verbis quae tamen evoluta continet amplissimam doctrinam: ἄρχων ἐστὶ φύλαξ νόμων.'

[5] Cf. ibid.: 'cum autem Magistratus pius vere sit membrum Ecclesiae.'

The *ius circa sacra* which thus belongs to the sovereign must needs include the suppression of heresy and the punishment of heretics:[1] 'Est autem potestas civilis pars Ecclesiae' (*CR*, 12, 497). And from the patriarchal character of the government the convenient parallel can be drawn that 'sicut quilibet paterfamilias minister et executor est Ecclesiae in sua familia... sic magistratus in republica minister et executor est Ecclesiae' (16, 124). The connecting line is 'omnes enim debemus obedire ministerio verbi'. So the common priesthood of all believers serves as basis for the historic alliance between throne and altar, and the same Melanchthon whose Alpha and Omega had been 'nos diligenter igitur observemus maximum intervallum inter Evangelium et politicam esse' (16, 419) proves to be the first advocate of theocracy in Lutheranism.

The history of the Lutheran Church in the next four hundred years in Germany is to a very large extent the history of Caesar's exploitation of what the Christian citizens were willing to render unto him. It is now, in retrospect, easy to see which were the most tempting concessions to power offered by Melanchthon: the touch of 'numen' and 'fatum' in his picture of the State;[2] the vindication to the magistrates of the 'custodia primae tabulae'[3] with the implicit distinction between 'interna' and 'externa' in the Church; and the invitation to the princes to serve as 'executors' in place of the episcopate failing in its duty.[4] Not only did the Nazi regime make the utmost use of these points in order to dress up its Church policy as genuinely Lutheran: the myth of blood and soil was the providential frame of national life, the decrees of Kerrl[5] were purely 'administrative' and left the 'inner' life of the Church 'intact', and the whole interference of the State

---

[1] See the following chapter.

[2] 'Divinae literae docent, divinitus praefici magistratus rebus politicis et fato principes dari', *CR*, 11, 91; the significance of this factor *for Luther* has been grossly overrated in Elert's *Morphology*.

[3] 'Nam et prima tabula propter disciplinam pertinet ad vitam corporalem', *CR*, 12, 697.

[4] 'Cum Episcopi non faciunt suum officium, debent Imperatores et Reges convocare Synodos', *CR*, 3, 472; anno 1537! Cf. the twenty-first of the Thirty-Nine Articles.

[5] The Nazi Minister for Church Affairs (whom Niemöller used to quote as 'Minister against Church affairs' and to hold responsible for the 'landes-kerrliche Kirchenregiment') inaugurated his policy of persecution under a number of amendments to a 'law for the security of the German Evangelical Church'.

ever since the appointment of a Church Commissioner (Jaeger) in 1933 was but an act of 'first aid' restoring the Church to its true peace and proper vocation.[1] But far worse, the Christians themselves found it exceedingly difficult to unmask and resist the subtle devil: in accepting National-Socialism as an expression of the *Schöpfungsordnung* (order of creation), many 'Lutheran' professors prostituted theology; in cooperating 'externally' with the Kerrl administration Zoellner experienced the great tragedy—so strangely similar to that of Melanchthon—of ending a life devoted to the freedom of the Church by handing it over to permanent State slavery; in maintaining the fatal idea of *Rechtshilfe* (legal aid) which even the Confessional Church thought right to expect from the government, the opposition wasted precious time and energy and gravely hampered its own struggle. *Die Staatskirche ist da* (This is the State Church) was the title of a pamphlet illegally published in 1936, and that sums up in four words the outcome of four centuries' 'concessions to power'.

Freed from the 'captivitas Babylonica' under the Papacy, the Lutheran Church in Germany woke up only to discover that it had exchanged one yoke for another, the clerical for the secular tyranny. It is no difference in principle whether the Church calls for the arm of the State or the State 'takes' the arm of the Church; in either case, as servant and as master, the magistrate is 'executor Ecclesiae'. The fault was not, as foreign critics have been eager to point out, to forget Christ's Lordship over Caesar; but, on the contrary, to conceive of Christ's Lordship in terms of Caesar. Calvinism, therefore, is no remedy; the Genevan establishment is but the reversal of the Roman; they are complementary forms of theocracy. 'It is not necessary for the Christian to assume without question that every political authority is being exercised in conformity with the vocation it has from God, and on which it is founded. On the other hand, he must not make arbitrary criticisms of the authority. Nor must he judge it according to

[1] Exactly the same is true of Nazi Church policy in Norway, where, in 1943, a Quisling Pastor 'had been asked to preach in Arendal to give the population an opportunity of hearing the Word of God clean and pure and not mixed with the usual politics and hatred' (*Vestlandske Tidende*, 24 May 1943, quoted in *Spiritual Issues of the War*, 1943, No. 188). Some years ago Goering boasted that the Nazi regime had led the Church back to a purely priestly and non-political ministry; the State, by taking over all the 'externa', had made the Church free to concentrate on 'pure religion'.

the Christian norms of his own life as a believer saved by Jesus Christ. He must judge it according to the biblical criteria for the State, seeking solely to discover whether it is or is not fulfilling its specific function as a state.'[1]

Here members of the French Protestant Youth Council have, under the lessons of persecution, sounded the note of true Lutheranism again. They have disentangled the confusion of the two powers in which Melanchthon and his successors became, in a very real sense, 'mixed up', and brought to light the 'maximum intervallum' between Church and State.[2] Neither domination nor imitation of the one by the other, but mutual responsibility marks their proper relationship. The 'executor Ecclesiae' is reduced to be the 'custos';[3] and the 'custody' is mutual, too. This step may be interpreted as the return from Melanchthon to Luther, albeit by way of simplification. For, however much the former could quote the latter as his authority, there are distinct signals of warning in Luther which in his absence and after his death were all too quickly overlooked. First, he was always aware of the provisional character of the 'Landeskirchentum'; the term 'summus episcopus' does not occur in his writings; he was confident that after the period of emergency the Church in a General Council would settle the 'reformation'. Secondly, he asserted and practised throughout his life the prophetic office of the Church in all public affairs. 'Doctor Martinus was asked whether a pastor or preacher had the power to criticize the authorities? Said he: Rather! For although it is God's order, yet God has reserved His right to judge the people and injustice.... But it behoves not a preacher to prescribe orders and to teach as to how dearly bread should be sold or meat be taxed.'[4] Thirdly, he knew human nature too well to have any illusions about the kingdoms and rulers of this world; a comparison of his personal reflections with those of Melanchthon would show plainly whose was the better psychology *and* eschatology. Lastly, and most important of all, he remained independent of all secular 'defensores fidei'; he detested Henry VIII for the assumption of that

[1] From 'Nation and State in the Bible', an article published on 18 February 1943 in *Le Christianisme au XXe Siècle*, quoted in *Spiritual Issues of the War*, 1943, No. 187.

[2] See above, p. 62.   [3] See above, p. 61.

[4] *WA Ti*, 5, 5257; cf. the Collect for the Day of St John the Baptist with the petition that we may 'after his example constantly speak the truth, boldly rebuke vice, and patiently suffer for the truth's sake'.

title;[1] and when his Saxon sovereign would not let him return unprotected from his Wartburg refuge to the dangers of Wittenberg, he gave the classic reply: 'I think I could protect your Electoral Grace more than you can protect me' (De Wette, II, 140).

Such were the safeguards which, in all his solidarity with Melanchthon, prevented Luther from *leaning* on power. He never allowed his 'concessions' to be forged into a final pact, or the Church to grow into a State, or vice versa. He did not dream of the 'Christian State', but was, in the words of the French document, 'seeking solely to discover whether it is or is not fulfilling its specific function as a State'. Once again the dualism of Law and Gospel, veiled by Melanchthon, appears in full clarity. Before vindicating the lawful authority of secular power Luther reminds the Christian that 'thou standest not in need of the powers for thy help, service or use, but rather they want thy help, service and use. I will have thee much too high and noble to want them; they shall want thee' (*WA*, XI, 254, 20 sq.). This makes him so extremely hesitant to consent to the actual use of force on the Christian side—even against an unruly ruler. Melanchthon was far less critical about the secular arm— be it in loyalty, or in resistance. He was, after all, the better politician.

B. CHURCH POLITICS

Brenz knew that when he wrote to him in 1549: 'Speras inveniri posse aliquem modum, quo et Christo et Caesareo *Interitui* [sc. Augustano] inserviri potest, hoc est, in his periculis quaerere modum, quo duobus dominis inter se pugnantibus servire possis' (*CR*, 7, 289). In the same letter the whole problem of Church politics is admirably stated: '... many are called, but few are chosen. Who are the many? The state. Who are the few? The Church. But the state is not in the Church, but the Church in the state; the state dominates, for it is the many; the Church submits, for it is the few. Therefore the Church has to bear what the state imposes, such as the ejection of the faithful teachers of the Church in order to restore idolatry and disturb discipline. Meanwhile the Church itself looks up to the Lord and expects deliverance' (ibid.). It may be questioned whether Melanchthon

---

[1] Cf. *WA Ti*, 4, 4694, 4699, 5152; *EA*, 28, 375.

was equally clear and candid about the minority status of the Church on earth, equally prepared to bear the consequences; it surely was a true description of his aim: 'in his periculis quaerere modum'. Since 'ecclesia est in civitate', the art of Church politics was for him to find a *modus vivendi* with the powers that be, with Pope, Emperor and Princes. Could he do that without being open to the charge of Brenz: 'faciamus...scandalosa, quo fiant bona' (ibid.)? Could he employ 'strong mail of craft and power' without rendering service to the prince of this world? In quoting Matt. vi, 24, Brenz had put his finger upon the fatal wound of all ecclesiastical diplomacy.

But Melanchthon had to 'establish' the Reformation. To him fell the task of representing the cause, while Luther was an exile in the Reich, and to guard his inheritance after 'Elijah' had passed away in 1546. The eyes—the very critical eyes—of Protestantism were upon him all the time; they (Luther, Brenz, Flacius) watched, while he had, in a very real sense, to 'play the game'. Luther's intuition saw the hand of Providence in this assignment: 'movent eum illa grandia reipublicae et religionis. Me privata tantum premunt. Sic sunt varia dona.'[1] And the diversity of gifts required diversity of character. The historian of the Augsburg Confession, C. A. Salig, was not mistaken in his diagnosis: 'Luther's greatest concern was about Philip Melanchthon. He was an excellent vessel and useful to employ in the Church; indeed the Augsburg Confession need not be ashamed of such a good labourer. But he was lacking the boldness of faith and the heart of Luther.... Melanchthon had charity and sought truth. The latter he meant not to endanger if he clung to the former.'[2] In another place we hear of the illuminating remark made by a contemporary: it was one thing to explain the cross in theology, but another to suffer it in practice and experience; to which Melanchthon replied: true enough, 'sed quis tandem erit finis praesentium mutationum et calamitatum?'[3] He was not made for resistance and martyrdom, but for conference and negotiation; by temper and tradition he inclined towards the humanist ideal of reunion, and many ties of personal friendship bound him to

[1] See above, p. xix.
[2] *Vollständige Historie der Augsburgischen Confession*, Halle, 1730, I, 203, 492.
[3] Ibid. p. 614. Cf. Ratzeberger, *Geschichte über Luther und seine Zeit*, ed. Neudecker, Jena, 1850, p. 180.

the party of Erasmus.[1] While he shares Luther's conviction that 'to deal with Zwingli is quite fruitless' (Melanchthon's words, *CR*, 1, 1066), he maintains the closest contact with Oecolampadius[2] throughout the critical days of Marburg in 1529 and writes to him in a revealing confession: 'Atque utinam ea essent tempora, ut frui hac nostra amicitia possemus. Sed incidit horribilis dissensio de Coena Domini....Itaque si quid in me desideras officii, tempora magis quam fidem meam accusare velim' (1, 1048).

Marburg is followed by Augsburg. Here the confessor prevails over the humanist, Luther over Erasmus; it was a true victory of the spirit over the flesh in him—as he once said in an entirely different connection: 'heroici motus sunt motus supra humanam naturam' (15, 567)—and it earned him the unqualified approval of Luther and the admiration of the spectators.[3] Yet it was a costly victory, reached through phases of defeatism and threatened by the danger of subsequent relaxation on Melanchthon's part. The picture of Augsburg is not complete without those recurrent temptations to overstep his competence and to put out private peace feelers of which the letter to Campeggio, the Papal Nuncio, is the most notorious. In it Melanchthon goes as far as this: 'We have no dogma different from the Roman Church....We are prepared to obey the Roman Church, if only she with the clemency which she has always used towards all peoples, would modify or relax some few matters which we, even if we would, could not alter....It is but a slight diversity of rites which seems to stand in the way of concord. But the canons themselves say that the concord of the church can be retained even with such diversity of rites' (2, 170). Such treatment of the *Augustana* is hardly better than Newman's interpretation of the Thirty-Nine Articles, and very much less pardonable. No wonder that the reaction of the faithful was 'not at all satisfied with such lukewarmness'.[4] Under the same heading must be recorded the

---

[1] See above, pp. 17 sq.; cf. R. Stupperich, *Der Humanismus und die Wiedervereinigung der Konfessionen*, 1936, pp. 20 sqq.; *CR*, 1, 63, 1083; 3, 68; 11, 15 sq.; 20, 701; 12, 269; 2, 709, 713, 776; 21, 440 sq.; Kolde, *Analecta Lutherana*, p. 279.

[2] Professor, Pastor and Reformer at Basle and Zwingli's partner in the sacramental controversy and the Marburg discussions with Luther and Melanchthon.

[3] See above, p. xvii. The Nürnberg delegates wrote home: 'and although Dr Eck and Philippus sometimes want to be heated against one another, yet the princes intervene on the side of moderation', *CR*, 2, 288.

[4] 'Mit sothaner Lauligkeit gar nicht zufrieden', Salig, op. cit. 1, 524, in another context.

attempts to reduce the whole issue with Rome to the three abuses 'de missa, de utraque specie, de coniugio sacerdotum' (cf. *CR*, 2, 122 sq., 149, 247 sq.), and, at the time of the Augsburg Interim (1548), to dismiss the doctrinal controversy about grace and faith in a parenthesis: 'Tamen non consulo, ut propter ambages verborum generaliores haec pars de doctrina reiiciatur.'[1] When in 1556 a visit to the King of France was invited and considered, Protestant feeling in authoritative quarters was that 'Melanchthon's articles would harm rather than help the Lutheran cause' and 'if one allowed him to reform by himself, he would produce a true Corinthian ore, i.e. gold, silver, copper and other metals would be mixed so that the outcome would be a "spotted" religion of Papal, Zwinglian, Lutheran elements with admixtures of his own'![2] In plain English, the suspicion was that Melanchthon's concessions to diplomacy would result in 'muddle'. All the more so since he was not infallible in his political instinct. He had strange illusions about the 'mansuetissimum Caesaris pectus' (*CR*, 2, 197); 'neque quicquam in tota aula est mitius ipso Caesare' (2, 122), he writes from Augsburg, and even as late as 1548: 'tanta est Caroli Imperatoris pietas, ut sanare et coniugare Ecclesias velit; credo, imperatoris voluntatem bonam esse, et video mediocres conditiones proponi' (6, 882; cf. 2, 254). To us this language sounds familiar enough; it is in exactly the same terms that certain churchmen and statesmen, both inside and outside Germany, pleaded the innocence and goodwill of 'the Leader' in the church crisis of 1933! The parallel will have to be studied more closely later on. Meanwhile, Melanchthon did not forget to consult his beloved astrology about the signs of the time and to read in the stars the course which the Emperor's life was to take (*CR*, 7, 759, etc.).

Here lies perhaps the key to his curious zigzag moves. That he was capable of secretly soothing Campeggio and publicly offending Eck (2, 288, 299); of befriending Oecolampadius and ignoring Zwingli; of producing the Augsburg Confession and defending the Interim; of accepting Bucer's tactics and refusing to go to Trent;[3] of sacrificing everything 'propter publicam Ecclesiae tranquillitatem et concordiam' (2, 328) and yet 'for no cause,

---

[1] *CR*, 6, 840.   [2] Salig, op. cit. II, 242 sq.
[3] 'Ursach, warum die Stände der A.C. das Tridenter Concilium nicht besuchen wollen', Feb. 1546; cf. Salig, op. cit. I, 545; Walch, *Luther*, XVII, 1112.

peace, war or reformation to abandon the true doctrine' (4, 428);
of offering in one and the same sentence 'zu compariren cum
asseveratione und doch protestieren dass man sich jetzund darein
nicht verpflichte...' (2, 655)—all this can only be explained by
assuming that he was on the look-out for the 'constellation' of
the hour to which to adapt his actions. Astrology, of course, is
only *one* illustrative factor in the general tendency, 'in his periculis
quaerere modum', to seek a middle way between 'love' and
'truth', to blame the circumstances rather than the people,[1] and
to make both sides in the struggle 'temporibus cedere'.[2] The
attitude towards the Emperor is no exception to this rule.
Melanchthon had gone a very long way to win his favour for
the Protestant cause; he specially asked Luther from Augsburg,
as indeed Luther had asked his Wittenberg congregation, to support his endeavours with their prayers; he tried his utmost, faithful
to the letter of the *Minor Catechism*, 'illum excusemus, bene de
eo sentiamus et loquamur, et omnia in meliorem partem acci-
piamus et interpretemur'.[3] When at last he saw that he had failed,
he had no final difficulty in abandoning what was no longer
'authority' in the biblical sense, and persuading himself that it
was his duty to make common cause with the princes even against
the Sovereign. It was a case not of breaking principles, but of
changing allies; and to find the right allies for the Gospel was,
after all, the very essence of his Church politics. 'Bündnis und
Bekenntnis' (Alliance and Confession) became, as H. von Schubert has shown, the *Leitmotiv* of Protestant history in the 1530's.[4]

Now it is precisely at this point that Luther launches his
vehement protests against Melanchthon's 'concessions'. 'Woe to
them that go down to Egypt for help; and stay on horses, and
trust in chariots, because they are many...but they look not
unto the Holy One of Israel, neither seek the Lord! Now the
Egyptians are men, and not God; and their horses flesh, and not

[1] See above, pp. 67 sq.
[2] *CR*, 2, 248, in the letter to Campeggio. C. W. Hering in his *Geschichte
der kirchlichen Unionsversuche* (Leipzig, 1836, 1, 195, No. 1) records a story
taken from Abraham Scultet's autobiography and traced back to Peucer,
Melanchthon's son-in-law; according to which Melanchthon, referring to
the change in his sacramental doctrine under the influence of Oecolampadius,
is supposed to have said in his family circle: 'if only I could be braver in this
defence (sc. the oral reception of the body of Christ), but in these times
and among these people it is impossible.'
[3] Eighth Commandment; see J. T. Müller's edition, op. cit. p. 355.
[4] *Schriften des Vereins für Reformationsgeschichte*, Leipzig, 1908.

spirit' (Is. xxxi, 1, 3). To seek for allies and to rely upon them was, in the prophet's sight, the fatal sin of Israel, and will be, in Luther's sight, the ruin of the true Church.[1] There is an unconfirmed story about a conversation between the two men in which Melanchthon hesitates to make a decision or undertake a journey because the position of Jupiter was not favourable; whereupon Luther exclaimed: what does it matter, when Christ is favourable! This is the answer to all 'astrology', and on this note the letters are written which Luther sent from the Coburg to guide his friend through the deep waters of the Augsburg Diet. Justus Jonas confirmed from Augsburg how much Melanchthon was in need of such comfort (*CR*, 2, 157); the periods when Luther in anger kept silence were unbearable (2, 140). In fact, Luther ridicules the notion, 'as if I sat here among roses and did not care about you' (De Wette, IV, 52); he had followed only too anxiously the fate of the Augsburg Confession and found that 'pro mea persona satis cessum est in ista Apologia' (ibid.); he suspects that the root of Melanchthon's troubles is 'not the magnitude of the cause, but the magnitude of our incredulity' (De Wette, IV, 49) and that 'Philosophia tua ita te vexat, non Theologia' (ibid.). Thus Melanchthon becomes his own greatest enemy, forging weapons for the devil and forgetting what is the only hope, namely, that 'Christ is not silent in the Diet'.[2] In the strength of Him who confesses us before His father in heaven, our only policy can be to witness a good confession: 'Ego vero dicam Philippo et nostris ut non disputent et contendant cum ipsis, sed simpliciter dicant: Haec est nostra confessio, hoc est verbum Dei; nos pollicemur omnem obedientiam corporum et bonorum; a verbo declinare non possumus; nisi per verbum aliter docemur. That is how I got through at Augsburg and Worms. Not so many disputations! One cannot do it that way.'[3]

[1] 'Sua quaerunt sub nomine evangelii, sed in periculis sibi timent. Nihil ad evangelium illa concordia politica. Deus est, qui servat et defendit in persecutione; huic fidamus et cum illo paciscamur foedus sempiternum. Mundus est Mundus', *WA Ti*, 3, 3830.   [2] De Wette, IV, 83.

[3] *WA Ti*, 4, 5040, p. 631, 1 sq. It is an interesting parallel to look at the letter which Calvin wrote to Melanchthon in 1550 and in which 'severius eius mollitatem et timiditatem in negotio adiaphoristico increpat' (*CR*, 41, 593 sqq.): 'Scio enim, quantopere inhumani rigoris crimen horreas. Sed memineris oportet, non maiorem Christi servis famae quam vitae rationem esse habendam. Neque enim Paulo meliores sumus, qui per infamiam et probra secure perrexit.... Nec vero vel mihi tu ita male notus es, vel ego tibi adeo sum iniquus, ut te ab aura populari ambitiosorum more pendere

'Ex eremo nostra' are most of these letters signed, and it is indeed the voice of one crying in the wilderness which speaks here, recalling his people from diplomacy to God and refusing to employ any other means in the propagation of the faith but the sword of the Spirit. The refusal is consistent; the secular arm must be avoided, be it as ally or as enemy of the Reformation. Hence Luther's inmost aversion to the military league against the Emperor;[1] and his desire, granted by Providence, not to see the outbreak of a religious war. 'We asked that His Grace (sc. Philipp von Hessen) would not, by this war, overthrow the doctrine of the Gospel or cause its name to be spoiled or break or grieve the common peace in the land' (*WA Ti*, 4, 5038); this is signed, with others, by Melanchthon and finds an echo in his lifelong anxiety 'quantum periculum futurum sit, si res ad arma deducatur' (*CR*, 2, 299). But Luther's motivation is strikingly different: 'lest through internal and civil wars, which are the worst of all, religion, policy and economy, God's Word, secular and domestic government be incessantly confused and confounded' (*WA Ti*, 4, 4352). It was the same apprehension which determined his attitude to the peasants' revolt: the fear of confusion between the power of God and the powers of this world. 'The Word, the Word, the Word must do it'—and the purity of this Word is at stake whenever the soldier of Jesus Christ 'entangleth himself with the affairs of this life'.[2]

---

arbitrer. Sed non dubito, quin te illae interdum punctiones debilitent. Quid? an prudentis et considerati hominis est, ecclesiam scindere ob res minutas et prope frivolas? Annon tolerabili aliquo incommodo pax redimenda? Cuius dementiae est, sic ad extremum tueri omnia, ut totius evangelii summa negligatur?...Neque hoc dico, quasi vel periculum sit, ne unquam tuo ministerio patefacta Dei veritas intereat, vel tuae perseverantiae ullo modo diffidam: sed quia nunquam satis sollicite cavebis, ne quam captant impii cavillandi occasionem ex tua facilitate arripiant....Imo non est quod testeris quam vehementer te crucient, sed quod dissimulas permulta quae corrigere non potes, vel non satis acriter et cordate resistis, id tuae humanitati non videri ipsis consentaneum nihil miror.' Cf. *CR*, 5, 735 and above, p. xxi.

[1] The Homily against Disobedience and Wilful Rebellion is strikingly Lutheran in its whole motivation and in its reference to the example of David who spared the life of Saul; 'lay no violent hand upon him, saith good David; but let him live until God appoint and work his end, either by natural death, or in war by lawful enemies, not by traitorous subjects' (New Edition, S.P.C.K. London, 1839, Second Part, p. 622).

[2] De Wette, I, 543: 'Nollem vi et caede pro Evangelio certari; ita scripsi ad hominem: Verbo victus est mundus, verbo servata est Ecclesia, etiam verbo reparabitur.'

The danger, on the other hand, is that the soldier, thus obeying the order of the day and defending his post, has no plan and strategy at all; that the Church becomes militant or 'Protestant' in a sterile sense, i.e. incapable of giving a lead for concrete decision and constructive action. It remains 'on guard' without making a move; it says No without pointing to a more excellent way. Evidently this danger has been acute in Lutheranism—though by no means only there—from the very beginning; we saw what could be made of Melanchthon's initial detachment of the Gospel from 'politics'. In Luther's case the original radicalism with which he views any league, alliance and rebellion against the Emperor (cf. *CR*, 6, 122) was bound to lose its savour from the moment when he left the question of the 'defensio licita' (6, 150) to the judgment of the experts; it was clear then that, albeit with very much greater hesitation, his signature would finally stand under Melanchthon's concessions to Church politics.[1] 'Isolationism' proved impracticable, even four hundred years ago, and in more than one particular sector; Luther had not only to advise and join Melanchthon, but to listen to Zwingli, to converse with Bucer, to conspire with the Princes, and even 'in eremo nostra', on the Coburg, he could not fail to realize daily the grim truth of 'ecclesia in civitate'.

These are eminently present-day issues, and the analogies between Melanchthon's diplomacy and certain aspects of the German Church conflict are worth pursuing. One cannot help comparing the 'cunctator' of 1530 with the Lutheran Bishops and the so-called 'Lutheran Council' of 1935 in their desperate attempt to 'settle' the dispute with the Third Reich; there the trust in the Emperor's bona fides (to separate him from the Papal party), here the pathetic assurances of loyalty to the 'Leader' (to make him disown the 'German Christians'); there the fear of the Gnesiolutherans, sometimes reaching hysterical heights,[2] here the horror and dislike of the 'Dahlemites' and 'Prussians'; there the confidential letters, the belief in negotiations, the drafts of compromise,[3] here the same atmosphere of secrecy and rumour,

[1] Cf. Elert, op. cit. II, 377; H. v. Schubert, op. cit. p. 28.

[2] *CR*, 7, 102: 'si putant inimici, ita se facturos concordiam et pacem, si meum sanguinem sorbeant, faciant quantum Deus permittet.'

[3] *CR*, 9, 68: 'so at Philippus' request they have put down some general and rather mild articles as a means of mediation for the consideration of either side, on the understanding, that either side should be entitled to add to, or leave out from, them, according to their several necessities.'

the regional blocks, the cooperation with the State Church Committees; in either case a mixture of timidity and genuine love of peace, a desire to save both one's own position and the unity of the Reich, and, above all, the supreme regard for the 'astrological' factor of the proper 'hour' before which no 'hasty' words must be spoken, no decisive steps be taken.[1] 'Usus sum mea Philosophia in qua non iam sum rudis tyro, hoc est tacui', writes Melanchthon (8, 724).

But others break the silence. 'We will suffer and abandon all that is in our power. But what is not in our power, they should, we pray, not expect from us; what is not God's Word, we have no power to accept, neither have we power to accept ordinances founded without the Word of God' (Luther, De Wette, IV, 143). There is a striking affinity between the voice from the Coburg and that of the prisoner in Sachsenhausen Camp. Under one of Niemöller's photographs the sentence is found: 'It is not for us to ask whether God's Word is true, but to believe that God's Word is God's Word and will do what it says.' He, unconsciously, is talking Luther's language, even in some details of style; he is at one with him and at variance with the 'Philippists' in all essential points: (a) in the disregard of diplomatic etiquette and tactics and the public appeal to the congregations; (b) in the fearless testimony before governors and kings; (c) in the conviction, which ever since has become part and parcel of the 'confessional' vocabulary, that God's Word is not in our power;[2] (d) in the refusal to commit the Church to any long-term policy, blue prints and peace aims, and the resolve to walk by faith and obedience from day to day.[3] And again, the cost and risk of this course—the protest without strategy—are conspicuous. Not that 'Niemöller was so careless' was the defect; it is to that very carelessness that his critics

[1] CR, 6, 945 (Cruciger about the Augsburg Interim): 'pro ratione temporis et hominum, quibus haec nunc scribuntur...satis graviter responsum esse'; note the contrast to Luther's 'satis cessum esse' with regard even to the Augsburg Confession, above, p. 70.

[2] Cf. such typical modern German phrases as 'es ist der Kirche verwehrt, eigenmächtig zu verfügen', etc.; and the significant coincidence that the decisive sentence, quoted by Luther in his letter to the Elector Prince, July 1530 (see above, p. 70), is the same on which Otto Dibelius preached in Dahlem after Niemöller's arrest in July 1937: 'but the Word of God is not bound.'

[3] In Pastor Niemöller and his Creed, Hodder and Stoughton, 1939, I have tried to give a personal account of the 'ecclesia militans' in Niemöller's ministry.

owe the safe enjoyment and continuation of their own livings. But the lack of 'planning' was painfully felt whenever the question of a new Church government was raised. The anathema against the 'German Christians', the non-cooperation with the State Church Committees, the rejection of disestablishment were mere negations (the last of these particularly unfortunate); 'unconditional surrender' is an impressive battle-cry, but it is no policy at all. Had not even Ludwig Müller, the Nazi Reich-Bishop, been quick enough to proclaim that a concordat was quite unnecessary in what he called an atmosphere of complete confidence between the new State and Church? The congregations rightly demanded to know where the hard struggle was going to lead them; and direction, both in the spiritual and technical sense, became ever more difficult with the progressive perfection of the enemy's method of persecution. In the end, resistance centred inevitably round the so-called 'intact' Churches, and the succession of Niemöller fell to Wurm, whose record had been decidedly 'Melanchthonian' and who now in his late seventies surprised friend and foe by the vigour of his fight. So far[1] the last chapter is still unwritten, and a league against the brown 'Emperor' has not yet officially been formed; the national emergency of invasion from East or West (the new *Türkenkrieg*) is all to his advantage and gives him the chance of silencing the opposition—no less brutally than before—in the service of the Reich. Yet things are moving under the surface, and the Church driven to the catacombs is at least in active neighbourly contact with the secular 'underground movement'; while from the borders of the Third Reich (and occupied Europe) the allied 'crusade' is encouraged by the same prophets who taught only yesterday that even the appearance of the British fleet in Hamburg could not help the Christian cause in Germany. 'Concessions to Church Politics' all along the front!

Has then Luther given in to Melanchthon? Or where is the limit to the concessions? It is obviously set by the Augsburg Confession. 'Bündnis' must be based on, and preceded by, 'Bekenntnis'. That is the declared policy of the Reformers to which the practice of the sixteenth century corresponds; the political pacts are signed over theological statements. The Zwinglians can therefore not be party to the League of Smalkalden (see *CR*, 5, 720), neither can an alliance with Henry VIII be

[1] Written in 1943.

concluded if his representatives refuse to subscribe to the *Augustana*.[1] Never did Melanchthon earn greater praise than when Luther wrote to the Elector Prince: 'Melanchthon and ours have maintained our dear Confession and did abide firmly by it, even if everything else went wrong';[2] but never was the need greater to watch him than at that very moment: 'So the Landgraf, too, made it clear to Philippus, not to give up what could not be conceded before God and one's conscience, but to abide by the truth, and thus by the Confession, Apologia and Articles of Smalkalden' (4, 256). For it was just then, in the days of Regensburg, that Melanchthon most gravely imperilled the fruits of the victory which the Spirit had won over his flesh at Augsburg;[3] in 1540 he produced the ominous edition known as *Augustana Variata*, and Luther had to remind him: 'Philippus, the book is not your, but the Church's Confession, therefore you have no power to alter it so often.'[4] So the original wording had to be restored.[5] Associates to the cause were welcome, even aliens from the highways and hedges might come in, so that the family of the 'Confessionsverwandten' might grow, but the arms of the family, the confession once made, could not be allowed to be changed. 'Amicus Plato, sed magis amica veritas' (*WA*, XVIII, 610, 10).

In very much the same way 'Barmen' has become the password for the 'radical' section of the Confessing Church since that great synod was held in 1934; here were the conditions laid down for the new order of the Church which no political necessi-

---

[1] See *CR*, 3, 927 sq. Smyth, *Cranmer and the Reformation*, pp. 34–48. H. E. Jacobs, *The Lutheran Movement in England*, 1891, pp. 167, 193. Luther (De Wette, IV, 688) writes to the Vice-Chancellor Burkhard in 1536: 'It is true that one must have patience if in England they cannot so suddenly put everything into practice according to the doctrine (as indeed it did not happen with us, either). But the chief articles must not be altered or abandoned. Ceremonies are temporal matters.... Whether or not to conclude the alliance with the King, in case he should not agree with us on all articles, I leave to your and His Grace's consideration as it is a secular affair; but in my opinion it is dangerous to unite externally where the hearts are not at one.'

[2] See above, p. xxi, note 1; Salig, op. cit. I, 516.

[3] See above, p. 67. The three conferences between mediating Protestant and Roman theologians concerned with 'Interim' solutions and deferring the war of Smalkalden (1546) took place in 1540–1 at Hagenau, Worms and Regensburg, and were all attended by Melanchthon.

[4] I have not been able to trace this quotation back to the Weimar edition; it occurs in Salig, op. cit. I, 494; Galle, op. cit. p. 420, note 2; E. S. Cyprian, *Historie der Augsburgischen Confession*, Gotha, 1730, p. 150.

[5] Salig, ibid. I, 521.

ties could modify or supersede. Any agreement was to be founded on doctrine; no other unity could be considered; and the official pulpit pronouncements even on current events were severely theological. So far from deliberate 'interference in state affairs' (where, on the contrary, many things were left undone which ought to have been done) the Confessing Church tried to view every detail of Church politics in the light of the eternal Word; an attitude beautifully expressed by Pierre de Bérulle, the French Cardinal and statesman, when he embarked for England on a highly diplomatic mission: 'We therefore ought now to worship God, who sent His Son into the world, because that mission is the sacramental prototype of all other missions. Without the great mystery of the Incarnation, whereby the Father sends His Son on a mission, there is nothing that can be acceptable to Him, for in the alternative it is ourselves or the Devil that inspires it. It is that great mission, and none other, that ought to constitute our motive.'[1] In other words, God cannot be left out even of ecclesiastical diplomacy;[2] the Gospel cannot be suspended; it is true in this sphere of life as everywhere else: 'without me ye can do nothing' (John xv, 5).

But are there not other things which can be, and indeed ought to be, left out, offences which could be avoided because they are not essential to the Gospel? This was what Melanchthon asked himself and his Church, when in Art. X of the *Augustana Variata* he deleted the Anathema ('et improbant secus docentes') and revised the formula for the real presence so that the text would seem acceptable both to the Roman and the Calvinist counterpart. In fact he secured the signature of Calvin to the new document,[3] causing the same grievance to the 'Gnesiolutherans' as was felt by Professor Sasse in 1934, whose full approval of the 'Barmen' declaration came to a sudden end when the Reformed members of the synod had agreed to it. Luther's own position

[1] *Histoire Littéraire du Sentiment Religieux en France*, par Henri Brémond, vol. III, La Conquête Mystique, l'Ecole Française, pp. 41 sqq., Paris, 1921.

[2] See George Glasgow, *Diplomacy and God*, Longmans, 1941, pp. 133 sq., from which the above quotation is taken.

[3] *CR*, 44, 428 sq.: 'Nec vero Augustanam Confessionem repudio, cui pridem volens ac lubens subscripsi, sicuti eam auctor ipse interpretatus.' 43, 211 sq.: 'Si hodie viveret eximius ille Dei servus, et fidelis ecclesiae, D. Martinus Lutherus, non tam esset acerbus vel implacabilis, quin libenter admitteret hanc confessionem.' 38, 331: 'De ipso Philippo nihil dubito, quin penitus nobiscum sentiat.' Cf. also 45, 148 sq.

is not so clear. Salig, the historian of the Augsburg Confession, tries his utmost to dissociate him from Melanchthon and again Melanchthon from Calvin;[1] but a full inquiry into Luther's utterances on the various editions both of the *Augustana* and the *Loci* would show as many pros as cons in each single case. No wonder that Melanchthon made use of this conflicting evidence in quoting to Luther his own words;[2] and that the *Variata* could 'happen' without, at any rate, a final break between the two friends.[3] We saw in the introductory chapter (above, p. xvi) how narrowly Melanchthon escaped Luther's public censure; and even before a *Variata* existed, the Elector Prince of Saxony was greatly alarmed by certain minor corrections in the 1537 edition, and, in a letter to Luther and Bugenhagen, faced the prospect of an ultimate choice between Melanchthon and the truth.[4] What was it then that prevented the crisis wherein 'the Lutheran Church would have lost her Melanchthon'?[5] How far is the *Augustana* variable and how far variety permissible within the one Church? It is the question of the nature and weight of credal formulae as such to which all Church politics point in the end and upon which depends the place for Melanchthon in Lutheranism.

[1] Op. cit. I, 475–92, 525 sq., 556–68.
[2] Ibid. I, 486, 525, 558.
[3] Cf. Kolde's article on the Augsburg Confession in Hauck's *Realenzyklopädie*, II, 249; and *CR*, 3, 366; 4, 437.
[4] See above, pp. xv sq.; *CR*, 3, 365 sq.
[5] Salig, op. cit. I, 483.

CHAPTER V

CONCESSIONS TO OPPOSITION

A. ADIAPHORA[1]

At the beginning of the last section we quoted Salig's description of Melanchthon's mind as divided between 'truth' and 'charity'. This applies not only in the moral sense—he was surely a mediator by nature—but it leads to a material consideration of what 'the middle' may be. Is there such a thing, or a complex of things, which can be defined as 'neutral' from the 'confessional' point of view, a No Man's Land between the fronts, issues on which opinions may differ and sacrifices be made for the benefit of the weaker brethren because they do not touch 'the faith'? In the language of the Formula Concordiae, it is the chapter 'de cere-moniis ecclesiasticis, quae vulgo adiaphora seu res mediae et indifferentes vocantur'. And it is, in the history of Protestantism, a long and stormy chapter. Melanchthon is involved from the very beginning. The Emperor, unable to suppress the Reforma-tion, tries to neutralize its effects by an 'Interim' solution, and a book is produced in 1548 which stabilizes the *status quo* and by which the Protestants to whom it makes a few concessions are forced to abide. The Articles of this ominous 'Augsburg Interim' are largely dressed up as 'adiaphora'. Flacius and the 'Gnesiolu-therans' denounce it in no uncertain terms and contest in par-ticular, as Luther had done (De Wette, IV, 83), the Emperor's right to decide such matters at all; they are sure 'that D. Martinus was no adiaphorist'[2] and that 'the other nations are being deterred from the Gospel, not by our stability, but by the in-

---

[1] For the definition of the term 'Adiaphora', see *CR*, 15, 1076: 'Et sunt adiaphora quae non sunt praecepta lege Morali'; 8, 841: 'Tandem Princeps nobis sua voce dixit: se non petere, ut doctrina mutetur aut ulla res necessaria, sed ut ritus externos in ordine festorum, lectionum, vestitu retinerent. Haec postea consiliarii nominarunt adiaphora. Nam ab ipsis vocabulum nobis initio propositum est. Sciebam, etiam levissimas mutationes ingratas fore populo. Tamen, cum doctrina retineretur integra, malui nostros hanc servitutem subire, quam deserere ministerium Evangelii; et idem consilium me Francis dedisse fateor. *Hoc feci: doctrinam confessionis nunquam mutavi.*' Cf. also 7, 357; and O. Ritschl, op. cit. II, 343, 345.

[2] Amsdorff, 1550.

stability of the adiaphorists';[1] but they are, as was to be expected, profoundly suspicious of Melanchthon's attitude, and a convention of the Saxonian Pastors at Coswig in 1557 draws up a statement to which he is asked to commit himself publicly.[2] Melanchthon, naturally, dislikes the procedure and is particularly nervous of the Flacian methods: 'Quod autem iam tantum mecum agitis de rixis Flacianis, quibus multas alienas caussas miscuit Flacius, scitis ipsi ad multos illa negotia pertinere, nec me sine offensione aliquid statuere posse. Si hoc agitur, ut ego opprimar, commendo me Deo et iudiciis piorum.'[3] O. Ritschl has, however, shown[4] that the black record in the controversial behaviour was not all on one side, and Melanchthon himself admitted: 'I confess to have sinned in this matter and I beg God's pardon for not having fled far from those insidious deliberations' (CR, 8, 842). But he would not go beyond such a personal gesture to an outright condemnation of 'Adiaphorism',[5] and the Coswig experiment failed. When the matter was finally settled it was long after Melanchthon had been delivered from the *rabies theologorum*,[6] in the Formula Concordiae, and the verdict meant essentially a victory for Flacius; Art. XI rejects the view 'cum asseritur, quod tempore persecutionis, quando clara confessio requiritur, hostibus evangelii in observatione eiusmodi rerum adiaphorarum gratificari et cum ipsis pacisci et consentire liceat, quae res cum detrimento veritatis coelestis coniuncta est'.[7]

Nevertheless, Melanchthon could claim that he had never subscribed to the Interim, even in its Leipzig version,[8] and apart from that, his comments on the Augsburg book, laid down in

[1] Westphal (Calvin's great antagonist in the sacramental controversy), 1551.   [2] Cf. above, p. 41, note 5.
[3] CR, 9, 62; cf. ibid. 68: 'But when they had arrived at Wittenberg and observed that they could not prevail upon Philippus in such ways... for he showed such gestures and excitement that they feared, if they insisted, his health might be affected.' 70: 'But the negotiators did not hand over this script to Philippus, giving as their reason that, if he received it, he might be all too angry.' See above, p. 72, note 2. Again CR, 9, 113: 'Scio Flacium non quaerere veritatem; ideo me Deo commendo.' 129: 'Ideo societas eius non est appetenda.' 146: 'Si Flaciana rabies me fugere coget, ostendet Deus alicubi hospitium', etc. etc.   [4] Op. cit. II, 1912, I, 359 sqq.
[5] See O. Ritschl, ibid. I, 361, 367; and, on the political implications, pp. 335 sqq.
[6] 'The Lutheran preachers all learn from Luther preaching and scolding, but they cannot learn from him to stop' (Melanchthon in *WA Ti*, 3, 3420).
[7] J. T. Müller's edition, p. 553, § 11.
[8] Cf. CR, 8, 840 and O. Ritschl, op. cit. p. 342.

four detailed 'iudicia', have a special interest for us.[1] 'A tolerable Christian Interim' is conceivable for him (*CR*, 6, 843, 855); he holds to what he had offered in his famous postscript to the *Articuli Smalcaldici*, namely, to tolerate episcopal and even papal jurisdiction on condition that the pure doctrine of the Gospel would be guaranteed (6, 840, 873, etc.; 2, 328); and he allows for a charitable and evangelical interpretation of the Mass as sacrifice (6, 857). But he contests the usurpation of the title 'catholic' by the Roman party (ibid. 840, 889); he suspects the Book for its many generalizations (839 sqq.); he fears that its outcome will be a new wave of persecutions (853, 875), for no 'patchwork' of this kind can ever lead to a lasting peace (4, 437). And however passionate he was in his concern for peace, however untiring in his admonitions to both sides that first things ought to be put first (6, 842, etc.), he would not stand for any dictated terms and any betrayal of the newly won 'libertas Christiana' (6, 843, 875, 941). 'We cannot and must not alter the Gospel of faith' (6, 875). It was truly a case of Psalm xi, 3: 'for the foundations will be cast down; and what can the righteous do?'

In this particular sense, then, Melanchthon might be called a 'fundamentalist'. The 'foundations' of the faith have to be defended at all costs; 'concessions' can only be made in adiaphoris.[2] The same mind which is 'open' on the latter point must needs be very definitely 'made up' on the former; so we must not be surprised to find Melanchthon adamant in all his dealings with real heresy. When, for example, in the case of Servetus, the Trinity is denied it is obvious that the very essence of the doctrine is at stake; it is a danger amounting to open rebellion and threatening the State as much as the Church; and the Genevan magistrates are to be congratulated on their firm and swift action: 'Dedit vero et Genovensis Reipublicae Magistratus ante annos quatuor punitae insanabilis blasphemiae adversus filium Dei, sublato Serveto Arragone pium et memorabile ad omnem posteritatem exemplum' (9, 133; cf. 8, 362; 24, 501). Mörlin, the chief opponent of Osiander, expresses similar satisfaction at the beheading of an Osiandrist.[3] In fact, Melanchthon had never any

[1] *CR*, 6, 839 sq., 853 sq., 865 sq., 924 sq.
[2] *CR*, 7, 385: 'Semper autem aliqua est Ecclesiae servitus, alibi mitior, alibi durior, ac leniri aerumnas servitutis consolatione vestra decet, non augeri condemnatione, *dum fundamentum tenemus*.'
[3] See O. Ritschl, op. cit. II, 368.

doubt 'de hereticis puniendis per Magistratum' (12, 696 sq.); his
decisive argument is: 'Never mind that some people say, faith
is not in our power. For it is not faith which is punished but
the heresy, that is the profession of a certain dogma, which is
in our power as much as other external delicts.'[1] Excommunication (16, 482 sq.) is to be distinguished from all secular punish-
ments; it is a spiritual weapon of the Church, but as such 'efficax
et divinum fulmen'.[2] It is the theory of the 'ius circa sacra' and
'ius in sacra' and the role of the magistrate as executor ecclesiae
(see above, p. 62) which is thus put into practice.

Once the son of perdition in his undisguised forms is ruled
out, the harder task begins of drawing the line of division between
the 'essentials' and 'non-essentials' and of defining more closely
what is meant by the 'foundations'. The obvious counterpart
to 'hereticus' is 'catholicus', and a typical Melanchthonian statement of that is: 'non legunt sapienter haeretici, qui non ex ipsis
fontibus hauriunt sententias, sed adferunt suae quaedam somnia:
deinde excerpunt mutila dicta, quae transformant in alienas
sententias' (CR, 11, 899). Departure from the 'fontes' and dis-
section of the 'corpus doctrinae' are, as we have seen before
(Chapter II, B), the chief crimes of the heretic; once again the
denunciation of the Schwärmer's 'somnia' brings Melanchthon
into closer contact with the 'old' Church.[3] And that is precisely
the company which he desires. It is of the greatest moment that
the *Confessio Augustana* in its very first article opens a common
front with Rome against the Manichaeans, Valentinians, Arians,
Eunomians, Mahometans, Samosatans 'et omnes horum similes';
that at the beginning of the second part Melanchthon is able to
make the solemn declaration 'cum ecclesiae apud nos de nullo
articulo fidei dissentiant ab ecclesia catholica';[4] and that Luther
follows his example in the *Articuli Smalcaldici*, the first part of

---

[1] *CR*, 12, 697; cf. 25, 56; 2, 710: 'Primum de seditiosis doctrinis non
opinor ambigi; certe Magistratui commissa est tutela pacis publicae, quare
non debet tolerare eos, qui spargunt dogmata, quae dissolvunt civilem
civitatem, qualia sunt Anabaptistica de Platonica communione rerum, de
non iurando, de non exercendis iudiciis, de non adeundis Magistratibus, de
coniugiis non rebaptizatorum etc.... Idem iudicandum est de his, qui etiamsi
non habent seditiosa dogmata, tamen per seditionem impetum in alios
faciunt....' See also above, p. 56, note 2.
[2] *CR*, 15, 1072, in connection with 1 Cor. v.
[3] 'Die Altgläubigen'; cf. above, p. 60.
[4] J. T. Müller's edition, p. 48, § 1; see also above, p. 67.

which, 'de summis articulis divinae maiestatis' (Trinity and Christology), simply states 'de his articulis nulla est inter nos et adversarios controversia, quum illos utrinque confiteamur; quamobrem non est necesse, ut pluribus iam de illis agamus'.[1] The 'foundations' are therefore summed up in the oecumenical symbols, Apostolicum, Nicenum, Athanasianum; they and the 'fathers' provide the basis for a true 'consensus doctrinae'; and the more the divided Church concentrates on the 'essentials' of the common faith, leaving room for disagreement on 'adiaphora', the more hopeful are the prospects of reunion (CR, 3, 514, 536). Here Melanchthon stands in the great humanist tradition which is continued by Bucer, Calixtus, Duräus, Grotius and Leibniz, which looks out for the 'Wesen des Christentums' beyond the 'confessions' (denominations) and which is eager to proclaim: 'in necessariis unitas, in dubiis libertas, in omnibus caritas.'

Before sounding Luther's reactions, we will in passing listen to some of Calvin's comments upon this subject. His 'oecumenical' interest which made him write to Cranmer that the cause of unity was worth the crossing of ten oceans[2] is as significant as his unchanging admiration and affection for Melanchthon. 'Literis tuis...nihil potuit accidere hoc tempore gratius'[3] is one of the typical opening phrases of their correspondence. And Calvin is prepared to go much further: 'Equidem non ignoro, si quid detur hominum auctoritati, longe aequius esse, ut tibi subscribam, quam ut tu in sententiam meam descendas.'[4] Yet the eyes which are thus fixed on Melanchthon cannot be blinded by friendship; they must be watchful and critical just because he is the man to whom multitudes of Protestants look up for guidance.[5] Three temptations in particular must be pointed out to him: ambiguity,[6] timidity and false

---

[1] J. T. Müller's edition, p. 299; see above, p. 12.

[2] CR, 42, 313 sq.: 'Atque utinam impetrari posset, ut in locum aliquem docti et graves viri ex praecipuis ecclesiis coirent, ac singulis fidei capitibus diligenter excussis, de communi omnium sententia certam posteris traderent scripturae doctrinam.... Quantum ad me attinet, si quis mei usus fore videtur, ne decem quidem maria, si opus sit, ob eam rem traiicere pigeat.'

[3] *Philippi Melanchthonis epistolae*, ed. H. E. Bindseil, Halle, 1874, p. 332.

[4] Ibid. p. 334.   [5] Ibid. p. 365.

[6] Ibid.: 'An hodie ignoras, plurimos ab ambigua illa, in qua te nimis timide contines, docendi forma dubios pendere?' Melanchthon himself admits in the *Acta Wormaciensia* (petitio dimissionis): 'In omnibus negociis ac praecipue in condemnationibus vitanda est ambiguitas' (not in CR).

moderation,[1] and an overdose of 'philosophy' in his doctrine.[2] In the case of the Adiaphora, Calvin's considered judgment was: 'This is the sum of your defence: if only the purity of doctrine be retained, there is no need to fight tenaciously about external things. Atque si verum est, quod pro certo passim asseritur, tu res medias et indifferentes nimis longe extendis.'[3] It cannot be quite accidental that in each of these few passages the crucial word of warning is 'nimis'.[4]

But how far can the concessions to adiaphora be extended? We consult Luther, and the first thing we learn is: 'My cause is not a "middle-cause" (Mittelhandel), in which one could modify, submit or give up, as I was fool enough to do so far' (De Wette, II, 244). This, we remember, is the note he struck in all his letters from the Coburg, and he refuses to take any blame for the breakdown of peace negotiations in Augsburg and since: 'We have made ample offers of peace and unity, Sed ipsi superbissime nolebant consentire' (WA, XXX, 3, 389, 14). Above all, in the question of the Mass there can be no compromise; as he reminds Melanchthon, even the King Hezekiah 'brake in pieces the brazen serpent that Moses had made, for unto those days the children of Israel did burn incense to it; and he called it Nehushtan (that is, a piece of brass)'.[5] Otherwise, of course, he is no fanatic and no iconoclast; when the *Augustana* states in Art. VII (and the Thirty-Nine Articles repeat it in No. 34) 'nec necesse est ubique similes traditiones humanas seu ritus aut ceremonias ab hominibus institutas', it only echoes that which Luther had said and practised in all his liturgical proposals and of which the famous letter to Buchholzer about vestments (De Wette, V, 234) is a delightful example. He knows the important distinction between 'Häuptsachen' and 'schweifenden Sachen' (cardinal and variable points); even among the prefaces to the New Testament is one about

---

[1] Ibid. pp. 417 sq.: 'etsi a turbulentis certaminibus abhorres, scis tamen quid suo exemplo Paulus omnibus Christi servis praescribat; certe maior tibi quam in eo spectata fuit, moderationis laus non est appetenda...ne tibi apud posteros dedecori sit taciturnitas.'

[2] Ibid. p. 334: 'me autem, ut ingenue fatear, religio impedit, ne tibi in hac doctrinae parte accedam; quod nimis philosophice de libero arbitrio disputare videris: in electione tractanda nihil aliud habere propositum, nisi ut te ad communem hominum sensum accomodes.'

[3] Ibid. p. 311.

[4] Cf. Mayer, *De nimia lenitate Melanchthonis*, Diss. 1695; H. A. Schumacher, *De timore Phil. Melanchthonis*, Grimma, 1730; and above, p. xx.

[5] 2 Kings xviii, 4. See Walch, *Luthers Schriften*, XVI, 1756 sq.

'which are the proper and principal books of the New Testament' (*WA*, Deutsche Bibel, vi, 10); but the principle of action is for him to achieve unity in the 'Häuptsachen' first and not to begin with concessions on the periphery.[1] 'If one is not agreed on the cardinal point, what is the use of giving or taking in those variable points? But if one were agreed on the cardinal point, we would be ready in the variable ones to give in, suffer and do what we should and what they like. For where Christ saves His own, we will gladly leave what is ours for His sake' (De Wette, iv, 95). It is not, however, always the quantity of agreement that decides the issue. In Marburg there were fourteen articles to which either side consented, and the difference about the eucharist was partial and cautiously worded; yet it was enough for Luther to tell Zwingli 'ye have another Spirit' (*WA*, xxx, 3, 150, 6 sq.). Similarly, in the case of reunion with Rome, the body of common doctrine must not be overrated. Kattenbusch has shown how 'Luthers Stellung zu den ökumenischen Symbolen' (1883) was to regard the faith of the Church as of one piece and not to recognize the mere subscription to the three articles if the work of God was not applied 'pro me'. The exposition of the Creed in the *Minor Catechism* makes this the central point, and in defining heresy Luther counts besides those who err either about the Godhead or the manhood of Christ a third class of those who do not let Him do His work.[2] To deny the justifying grace is to deprive Christ of His glory and, in fact, to have another God; the controversy about the 'sola fide' must needs be christological too, though in Luther's times it was not always stated in such terms. The sacrifice of the Mass as the embodiment of false doctrine is therefore an insuperable obstacle to unity. While allowance has to be made for the faithful 'under' the Pope as distinct from the papal system and while Luther is even ready to admit that 'nulla enim haeresis unquam fuit, quae non etiam vera aliqua dixerit, ideo vera non sunt neganda propter falsa' (*WA*, xiv, 694, 30), the general Anathema against the 'Antichrist' can never be silenced or suspended, not even in the act

---

[1] 'Let them first restore the doctrine of faith and works; then we shall see about the ceremonies. Let them return churches and ministers to their proper use, then the ordinances will look after themselves.' (Luther in an undated letter to Melanchthon, see Walch, *Luthers Schriften*, xvi, 1756 sq.)

[2] *WA*, L, 269, 1 sq. In the context the Papacy is accused of promoting the third heresy. Cf. also above, p. 17.

of prayer: 'for I cannot pray, without also cursing.... Am I to say: "Thy kingdom come", I must also say: "Cursed, condemned and destroyed be the Popery with all the kingdoms on earth which are against Thy kingdom"' (*WA*, XXX, 3, 470, 19 sq.). Here, indeed, is nothing left of Melanchthon's 'nimia ambiguitas' or 'taciturnitas'. On the other hand, Luther felt no need to indulge in the secular methods of inquisition or to express any sympathy with Calvin's treatment of Servetus. He has a slightly different conception of Christian love which is no less definite than his profession of faith and based on the same biblical source (Eph. iv): 'If we are to have Christian unity and Christian love with them, we also must love their doctrine and practice or at least suffer it. Whoever may do that—I won't. For Christian unity is in the Spirit, where we are of one faith, one heart, one mind.... But this we will do willingly: to be at one with them profanely, that is to keep external and secular peace; but spiritually we will avoid, condemn and punish them' (*WA*, XXIII, 85, 28 sq.). Unity in Spirit was a thing not to be forced, but to be awaited by faith. To Bucer who had made the cause of concord his 'business'—with all the good and bad marks of that word [1]—he wrote about the sacramental conflict: 'If this notion has not yet matured amongst you, I think we must leave it and wait for further divine grace. I cannot give it up, and even if, as you write, you don't feel that the words of Christ require it, yet my conscience feels that they do. Therefore I cannot profess a plain and solid concord with you, if I do not want to violate my conscience and moreover to sow the seed of much greater trouble in our churches and still sharper discord in the future, after having forced agreement in such a way now' (De Wette, IV, 216 sq.). No doubt this was 'speaking the truth in love' and indicating the 'middle' way for which Melanchthon had looked in another direction.

[1] From Kolde's article 'Regensburger Religionsgespräch' in Hauck's *Realenzyklopädie*, XVI, 546: 'It now was a question of winning the Protestant "estates" (Stände). One decided to send the book, through the mediation of the Elector Prince of Brandenburg, to the princes and to Luther, and Bucer advised Landgraf Philipp (von Hessen) to behave as if he saw it for the first time. With a covering note, very diplomatically worded by Bucer (10 January 1541), it was sent via Marburg to Johann II with the request to pass it on to Luther. Almost with the very words suggested by Bucer the Elector Prince sent it to Wittenberg on 4 February (cf. *CR*, 4, 92).' See Salig, op. cit. I, 414, 435, 524, 395.

A permanent register of Adiaphora is an obvious impossibility; the task of defining the boundaries rests with every new generation; and the general attitude towards heresy has completely changed since the times of the Interim. Not only is this true of the tone and style of polemics; few theologians are desirous of a return to the Flacian era; but the balance of the whole problem has been shifted. As Calvin observed, 'hodie vero non de circumcisione nobis molesti sunt hostes: sed ne quid sincerum nobis relinquant, putidis suis fermentis et doctrinam et omnia pietatis exercitia inficiunt'.[1] If the Reformers were so conscious of their own distance from the apostolic age, how much more must we realize the crudity of our contemporary heresies in contrast to four hundred years ago;[2] what is Servetus when compared with Rosenberg, and Leo X compared with Hitler! We can hardly think of the Vatican when we speak of the Antichrist to-day, neither do we find it easy to say with Luther that Zwingli's death in the battle of Kappel was the divine recompense for his sacramental errors. Not because we are children of the eighteenth and nineteenth century and have ceased to take such matters as the sacraments or the Antichrist seriously—on the contrary; but because in the footsteps of the Reformers and in the school of persecution we have learnt to see the 'Häuptsachen' and the 'schweifenden Sachen' in a new proportion. The Confessional Church was right when at its Halle Synod in 1937 it restated the relations of Lutherans and Calvinists as follows: the break between our fathers 400 years ago is no sufficient reason for continuous separation; the union between our fathers 100 years ago (by force of the State) is no sufficient reason for continuous intercommunion; viewing our differences in the light of scripture and searching for further illumination, we suggest that under the present circumstances no Calvinist shall be refused admission to a Lutheran Communion on the sole ground of his Calvinism, nor vice versa. Hans Asmussen was equally right in following up this synodical statement by a list of basic articles constituting a new 'consensus de doctrina evangelii' and of open controversial questions;[3] it was a procedure strictly parallel to the Marburg Articles. Finally, the Barmen Synod was supremely right when it concluded the joint declaration of its Lutheran and Reformed members with

---

[1] Bindseil, op. cit. p. 312.
[2] 'Profecto crassioribus corruptelis te manum dedisse', ibid.
[3] In *Abendmahlsgemeinschaft?*, München, 1937.

the sentence: 'We leave it to God what this may mean for the future relation of the two denominations.' That again was strictly in accordance with Luther's advice to Bucer (see above, p. 85).

Unfortunately, it is necessary to point out that to commend the cause of unity to God does not mean to 'stay put' and to refuse collaboration in oecumenicis. Official Lutheranism has all too often been guilty of such a quietist attitude, here as in other spheres; it pretended to take unity so seriously that it could do nothing about it—a pious disguise of sheer particularism which of course is found in more than one camp.[1] There is not the slightest reason to rejoice, as Elert does,[2] in the fact that except for the Roman Church the Lutherans (of the Missouri Synod) are the only body not associated with the Federal Council of Churches in America. Precisely because the Adiaphora are a variable factor in Church history, the frontiers which separated the fathers have to be re-examined; when this is done, it will be found that the true line of division does no longer coincide with the denominational boundaries.[3] If there remain essential articles of faith which keep us apart they must be worked out, and to this end the attendance of conferences on 'Faith and Order' as well as 'Life and Work' is indispensable. In the Reformers' life-long appeal to a General Council and in their distinction between the 'Häuptsachen' and the 'schweifenden Sachen' is a lesson and a challenge for us; even the Formula Concordiae in its Art. X starts from the assumption that there must be room for Adiaphora in the Church and quotes Irenaeus: 'dissonantia ieiunii non dissolvit consonantiam fidei' (in J. T. Müller's edition, p. 553, § 7).

To this extent, then, Melanchthon is vindicated. His error lay, as Calvin had noticed (see above, p. 83), in the tendency to extend the radius of the Adiaphora, or, to put it differently, to underrate their 'dynamic' character. 'In statu confessionis nihil est adiaphoron', insisted Flacius, and here the Formula Concordiae

[1] Albrecht Ritschl reports on 28 November, 1869, to the Minister von Mühler, that in his country people were 'in the first place Hanoverian and only in the second Lutheran' and that 'Lutheran Churchmanship was above all a symptom of political particularism' (see O. Ritschl, *Albrecht Ritschls Leben*, II, 73). Accordingly, Bishop Marahrens of Hanover said in a pastoral letter of 1935: 'It goes without saying that we regarded as our duty the strictest observance of the rules of the different counties—also a sign of sound Lutheranism' (!).

[2] Op. cit. II, 266–9.

[3] See Archbishop Temple's preface to the Lent Book, 1943, by Dr N. Micklem.

sided with him against the 'Philippists'; there is no detail of
doctrine or order, however peripheric and minute, which cannot
at any time, in a moment of crisis, become the 'articulus stantis
et cadentis ecclesiae'. The Antichrist has many incarnations—'si
non potest leo esse, vult esse draco'[1]—and one of his cunning
devices is to choose 'adiaphora' as targets in order to deceive
the faithful and to weaken their resistance. What time and pain
did it cost the Church in Germany to realize that the Gospel was
at stake when the conflict was about such trifles as collections,
notices, flags, etc.;[2] were these really objects worthy of risking the
safety of the pastor and the peace of the congregation? No wonder
that the majority felt as Melanchthon did: 'if our confession is
firm in the necessary things, one cannot find fault with us; in
the other matters, however, we will show our modesty and
tolerance in servitude; it is a greater scandal to desert the church
for minor causes than to give the adversaries some occasion to
revile our moderation...ut interea maneat Ecclesia in rebus
principalibus in eodem statu, et non tollatur ministerium Evangelii
et non turbetur invocatio in populo' (CR, 7, 324). The classical
reply to this argumentation is contained in Corvinus's angry
question: 'how can that be an adiaphoron which lands the
preachers in gaol?'[3] And there is the limit for all 'concessions'.
Had it been said before that the boundaries of the Church vary
in every generation, then it has to be said now that these boundaries must nevertheless be definite and visible. If the 'Confes-
sionalists' are apt to forget the one, the 'Adiaphorists' are apt
to forget the other. Lutheranism cannot leave it to Rome to
inquire and to decide what is 'intra' and what 'extra' ecclesiam.

B. DIAPHORA

But there is yet another line of division which we have to consider.
So far we were concerned with different sets of articles, with the
problem of a minimum of 'essentials' and a maximum of Adiaphora which could serve as lowest common denominator between
the Churches; to leave the heretics 'without', but to widen the
circle 'within', was Melanchthon's first contribution to unity.
How far must the Church be exclusive? was the question. It

[1] Luther, De Wette, IV, 155.   [2] Cf. above, p. 63.
[3] *Epistolae Mel.* ed. Bindseil, p. 297. Antonius Corvinus, the Reformer
of Brunswick, spent three years in prison for his protest against the Interim.

remains to ask: How far can it be comprehensive? Supposing the boundaries between 'extra' and 'intra' ecclesiam were settled and agreement reached about the Adiaphora, there would still be the friction between the various schools, types, parties within the one Church; divided not so much by a body of doctrine as by the mode of expressing the common faith. Diversity of language is the main factor in our 'Diaphora', a factor whose importance for Melanchthon we had already to note on more than one occasion (see above, pp. xxvi sq., 7, 17, 76 sq., etc.), and to recognize which is the chief concession to opposition 'inside'.

We remember Brenz's description of the Melanchthon-Osiander controversy as a 'bellum grammaticale' (see above, p. 51). Bucer took the same view of the sacramental dispute; 'he managed to mediate between them both so that what the Swiss called "verily" (wahrhaft), would mean "essentially" (wesenhaft) for Luther and the (Augsburg) Confession. Both he asked not to obstruct the concord because of the difference in words.'[1] A unionist of the nineteenth century was able to put it even more convincingly when pleading for the so-called Sacramentarians that they 'believed with equal, and often greater, intensity and sincerity and said: Christ is the true bread of life; only they could and would not say: the bread is the true Christ'.[2] Even Luther was attracted: 'that M. Bucerus maintains, the strife was about words alone: for that I would willingly die, if only it were so' (De Wette, IV, 219); and in the period immediately after the Wittenberg Concord (1536–7) his letters sound strangely irenical: 'wherein we do not fully understand each other, it is the best thing to be friendly towards, and believe the best of, one another, till the water be cleared' (ibid. v, 86). There was a moment when he was prepared to reduce the conflict between Melanchthon and Agricola to a matter of terminology (see above, p. 35);[3] and once he could talk about the dissenters in his own camp in truly Melanchthonian terms: 'ego soleo dissimulare et celare, quantum possum, ubi aliqui nostrum vere dissentiunt a nobis' (see above, p. xxi). Wesley, as we have seen (above, p. 48), uses the same discretion with regard to 'imputed righteousness' in his sermon on Jer.

[1] Salig, op. cit. I, 435; cf. ibid. pp. 390, 403, 416.
[2] C. W. Hering, *Geschichte der kirchl. Unionsbestrebungen*, Leipzig, 1836, I, 201.
[3] De Wette, III, 215: 'Scripsit similia fere Mag. Eislebius (sc. Agricola), sed ego pugnam istam verborum non magni puto, praesertim apud vulgum' (Luther to Melanchthon, 1527).

xxiii, 6: 'it is true, believers may not all speak alike; they may not all use the same language. It is not to be expected that they should.... We may go a step farther yet: Men may differ from us in their opinions, as well as their expressions, and nevertheless be partakers with us of the same precious faith.'[1] Conversely, 'etsi vera Ecclesia, quae est exigua, retinet articulos fidei, tamen illa ipsa vera Ecclesia potest habere errata, obscurantia articulos fidei; praeter ea multi ita labuntur...' (Melanchthon, CR, 23, 601).

If this is at all a fair picture of the situation—the quotations could be vastly supplemented—it follows that all 'dealings' of the Church with its own Diaphora must be guided by three principles.[2] First, thorough examination of the *real* reasons underlying the dissensions; 'saepe autem doctrinae consensus propter privatas discordias turbatur', writes Melanchthon warningly (CR, 15, 379); and the Edinburgh Conference on 'Faith and Order' was well advised to devote one whole volume of its report to the 'non-theological elements in the making and unmaking of church union'. Secondly, imaginative appreciation of the divine purpose behind our unhappy divisions; an instance of this is given in Brenz's retrospective remarks on the two main issues in the Reformation struggles: 'The struggle which broke out recently, about the blessed sacrament of Holy Communion, was in itself hostile enough. But the merciful God is so gracious not to let the struggle come to pass, if He had not intended thereby to illustrate and declare the true meaning of the sacrament.'[3] Thirdly, extreme care in all *ex cathedra* verdicts and avoidance of all generalizations (see CR, 7, 103 sq.; 9, 63 sq.); to quote the same source again: 'Temerarium igitur est iudicare, eum veram Ecclesiam et doctrinam eius deserere, qui non mox in illius aut istius ministri sententiam concedit, praesertim cum fieri possit, ut rixatores de quibus minister ille fert sententiam, utrique recte sentiant, si recte explicetur. Fieri enim potest, ut utrique errent.'[4]

---

[1] *Works*, v, 238; cf. ibid. VIII, 340, § 2: 'The Character of a Methodist.'

[2] CR, 1, 874: 'ἐπιείκειαν quam in Ecclesiasticis dissensionibus in primis praestari oportebat. Neque enim aliter aut conservari aut sarciri Ecclesiae concordia potest.' Cf. in more detail 16, 405, where Melanchthon quotes Deut. xxxii, 35, John xiii, 5, Luke vi, 37. Also 15, 337: 'Oriuntur enim dissidia ex his tribus fontibus, vel ex ignorantia, vel ex ambitione, vel ex impatientia.'

[3] S. Pressel, *Anecdota Brentiana*, p. 335. Similarly about justification.

[4] Ibid. p. 359. Cf. above, p. 30 and CR, 16, 405: 'Severitas pertinet ad officium, quod Dei est, non nostrum.... Non sumus iudices, quod ad privatas personas attinet, sed sumus Deo rei multipliciter.' Also CR, 2, 854, etc.

The many voices in the Church, none of which is without signification (1 Cor. xiv, 10), require therefore the gift of interpretation. Melanchthon is well aware of that: 'the gift of interpretation is with the true church, but not bound to certain persons or places; it is sometimes with the many, sometimes with the few, sometimes more, sometimes less lucid and pure.'[1] In its negations the statement is aimed at Rome; the Tridentinum and the Vaticanum provide the classical examples as to how *not* to try the spirits. Tempting and impressive as it sounds to have the seat of authority fixed in time and space, and every pending dispute infallibly settled for ever, it is a solution which must prove fatal because of its very secularism; in nature and method it ignores the distinction between iudicia politica and ecclesiastica (cf. *CR*, 15, 1347) and the fact that 'veritas non alligata ad maiorem numerum' (15, 1350; cf. 23, 603). Luther knew best how hard it could be to assert the latter point against the overwhelming majority of centuries of Christian tradition; but even that could not be allowed to influence the course of the Reformation. And Melanchthon with his infinitely greater conservatism and timidity indignantly denies a Flacian rumour: 'me dixisse, Non discedendum esse ab Ecclesiis, etiamsi omnes veteres abusus restituerentur, manifestum mendacium est' (7, 480); all he demands is 'oporteat dissentientes ab ordinaria potestate certos esse de veritate doctrinae, quam profitentur et amplectuntur' (14, 773; cf. 15, 38); but he has as little doubt as Luther that 'the pillar and ground of the truth', of which Paul speaks to Timothy, refers expressly to 'the church of the living God', i.e. the true Church throughout the ages, not the official 'synagogue' which usurps the title (cf. 15, 1345 sq.). More often than not the prophetic remnant is struggling against the Priests and Scribes and literally driven to an exodus;[2] this is no proof against, but for, the belief 'sciamus inter has confusiones tamen aliquam esse veram Ecclesiam et discamus ubi quaerenda sit, et nos ei adiungamus' (15, 1356). In particular, the voice of the Bishops must not be mistaken to represent the whole communion of saints: 'in controversiis de doctrina non debent soli Episcopi iudicare, sed eligendi sunt homines idonei ex toto corpore Ecclesiae' (3, 472). On one occasion, despite his usual willingness to come to terms with the

---

[1] *Acta Ratisbon* (not in *CR*), 1, De Ecclesia.
[2] Cf. *CR*, 23, 597: 'tamen sciendum est, hanc veram Ecclesiam non semper pariter florere, sed saepe admodum exiguam esse'; ibid. 601 sqq.

Episcopate (see above, p. 80), Melanchthon's scepticism is even greater than Luther's: theological examinations ought not to be entrusted to men whose doctrine is not 'safe' (*WA Ti*, 4, 4595–6). The synodical element is vital to the true order of the Church; herein the Princes, such as Constantine (*CR*, 3, 472; 11, 435), have shown more insight than the hierarchs and made good their right, nay, their duty to summon a synod where the Church authorities failed (ibid.; see above, p. 61). 'Nam cum Synodi totius Ecclesiae iudicia sunt, non tantum Episcoporum, concedenda sunt suffragia etiam aliis piis et doctis, qui non funguntur ministeriis ecclesiasticis' (*CR*, 11, 435; cf. 760). Of course the Reformers are used to being called schismatics;[1] but the charge, so far from frightening them, is turned back upon Rome itself. As Luther reminds the Bohemian brethren, it is not the Church but the tyrants of the Church whom they oppose (*WA*, VI, 504, 19 sq.), and it is better to lead a 'sectarian' life than to be 'united' under the tyranny of the Pope.[2]

The failure of totalitarianism in the Church may, as is only too plausible, induce other Christian bodies to despair of authority altogether, to abandon the function of doctrinal judgment and to proclaim *liberté, égalité, fraternité* in place of the 'confessions'. 'Der rechte Ring vermutlich ging verloren',[3] says Lessing's Nathan, the herald of modernism, refusing to choose between Christianity, Jewry and Islam. Whether the Diaphora as such appears as blessing or as curse, as a 'rich variety' of 'happy divisions' or as a mere 'bellum grammaticale' of brothers who all 'mean the same thing' is a matter of temperament rather than a difference in principle; in either case it would seem 'unchristian' to commit oneself to what can only be 'one side', and to condemn the other; the proper contribution to unity is to remain 'impartial'. That this kind of 'Protestantism' is not what our fathers meant, but a bad caricature, the Charybdis which they were as anxious to avoid as the Roman Scylla, need hardly be said; but

---

[1] See Melanchthon's report of his first encounter with Eck at Worms; see Postille, ed. Pezel, II, 118, quoted by Galle, op. cit. pp. 163 sq.

[2] *WA*, XII, 172, 6 sq.: 'Sic, inquam, melius est nullum habere quam sacrilegum, impium et sceleratum ministerium' ('Dehortatio a suscipiendis ordinibus papisticis', from *De instituendis ministris Ecclesiae*, 1523).

[3] 'The Jewish book Kuzair (twelfth century) said that Judaism, Christianity and Islam, are like three rings having such a close resemblance that one can hardly distinguish one from the other.' Lev Gillet, *Communion in the Messiah*, Lutterworth Press, 1942, p. 104.

it is worth noting the unusual determination with which Melanchthon meets the 'neutrals'. In a chapter 'de unitate Ecclesiae'
(part of a sermon on Luke xi, 14 sq.) he remarks: 'In all dissensions it happens that many when they see that there are some
errors on either side, take offence and withdraw, unwilling to join
either party. They pretend to have causes for suspending their
assent; they want to appear wiser and more moderate than the
others.... But Neutrals of this type are not excused, for by the
very fact of their neutrality they show that they have come into
doubt, and instead of seeking remedies against it, they nurse it,
till they finally abandon the faith. For he that is and remains
neutral, has no faith, as is written: he that gathereth not with me
scattereth abroad. Ideo Neutrales sciant, non satis esse tacere, sed
necessariam esse confessionem' (CR, 24, 500; 14, 855).

Even the Anglican offer of a via media could not be accepted
by the Reformers. Well-disposed as Melanchthon was towards
Henry VIII and his ambassadors, open to negotiation and almost
made for the Cambridge professorship, the fact remains and has
a symbolic meaning that he never crossed the channel, never was
'free' to follow in the footsteps of Bucer. The Augustana proved
an insuperable barrier (see above, p. 74); as long as the English
would not subscribe to it and retained so many 'abusus', the Ger-
mans were bound to suspect with Luther that the King only
'corpus papae occidere voluit, animam vero illius conservare
voluit, impiam doctrinam' (WA Ti, 4, 4694)—a suspicion which
to some extent has been justified by subsequent developments
of Anglicanism. 'Doctrine in the Church of England', as laid
down in the Report of the Archbishops' Commission of 1922
(published 1937), is 'comprehensive' in a measure which passeth
Lutheran understanding; the Thirty-Nine Articles in spite of
being solemnly read out by every incumbent after his induction
hold no place comparable to continental Confessions of Faith,
in fact they are openly renounced by large sections of the Anglican
Church. What makes the Diaphora tolerable is the common
basis of the Prayer Book, the Episcopate and the Establishment;
the underlying unity expresses itself in liturgy, order and constitution. Thus it is possible that 'Catholics' and 'Protestants' (and
many others) can live together under one roof and become pillars
of the same building; by retaining those elements of the tradition
which the continental Reformation abandoned as 'abusus' Anglicanism avoided schism and disruption and qualified for its present

'central' position as mediator in ecumenicis. Because it can speak of 'the appeal to antiquity as a principle of the English Reformation' (Kidd, 1901), it is able to lend special force and weight to its 'Call to Union on the Principles of the English Reformation' (W. F. Hook, London, 1838); and the claim is widely heard and recognized. The successful combination and collaboration of doctrinal extremes in the Establishment is a truly amazing achievement of statesmanship in which Archbishop Davidson was an unrivalled master; no one was more ready to pay him this tribute than Charles Gore: 'When I go up the stairs at Lambeth, I say, Charles, you be very careful. When I come down the stairs, I say, Charles, you know that you never meant to agree to that.'[1]

The Lutheran reaction to Lambeth may be stated in exactly the same words; only the practical conclusion is the opposite, namely, not to climb the stairs! 'Es muß uns die öffentliche wahrheit eynis machen, und nit die eygensynnickeit' insists Luther;[2] the doctrinal issue cannot be evaded. On the contrary, there may be variety in liturgy, order and constitution in the united Church, as the *Augustana* teaches,[3] and as the history of Lutheranism testifies; but doctrinal unity can never become an Adiaphoron—'grant that all they that do confess Thy holy Name may agree in the truth of Thy holy Word, and live in unity and godly love.' In a letter rejecting certain proposals connected with the Regensburg Interim Luther points out that compromise is no concord and that true reunion must be sought in reconciliation with God: 'if the Kaiser seriously wanted to promote concord and peace, it would have to be done with God or in God's Name. Which is in plain German: they would have to reconcile themselves with God and to confess in public that what they have done so far was too much of a good thing.'[4] Here we touch upon the 'articulus stantis et cadentis ecclesiae'; the quest for unity is at bottom the quest for the gracious God; and it is not incidental that the Church of Sweden in establishing intercommunion with the Church of England has laid decisive emphasis upon 'the recognition of Scripture as norma normans both with regard to life and doctrine, and the building of our salvation on God's

---

[1] G. K. A. Bell, *Randall Davidson*, II, 1160.
[2] 'The plain truth must make us one, not our own mind', *WA*, VI, 455, 14.
[3] See above, p. 83; *CR*, 12, 434, 484.
[4] De Wette, V, 376; ibid. p. 368 against a false idea of 'toleration'.

grace alone by faith'.[1] The authors of that declaration are, of course, aware that 'Biblicism' and 'Solifidianism' are but two aspects of the same thing, the one concerned with the authority, the other with the contents, of scripture; they are traditionally known as the formal and material principles of the Reformation.

But how is it possible to master the Diaphora on the doctrinal basis of this twofold principle? Again we have to begin with a negative statement. The control of tongues by the word of scripture does not mean that the true Church is committed to, or known by, the exclusive use of biblical language. Not that the danger of this particular exaggeration is very acute in these days of 'dialectical' and 'existential' theology; the growing estrangement of our modern technical jargon from the biblical vocabulary—already apparent in a comparison between, say, Wesley and Kierkegaard—is quite an alarming symptom. But Melanchthon in his 'studium proprietatis'[2] was all too anxious about uniformity of speech, partly for the benefit of his juvenile pupils,[3] partly for the sake of 'better understanding' in his many current controversies: 'in order to preserve unity we think fit not to mix alien disputations into this article so that the usual form of speech be retained' (CR, 9, 16). 'The usual form' did refer to the fathers[4] as much as to the Bible and produced that standardized phraseology which we found described by Melanchthon himself as 'semper eadem cantilena' (see above, pp. 11 sq., 30). Bucer tended towards a stricter Biblicism which should exclude all controversial terms (even 'Trinity'), prevent errors and secure a truly interdenominational basis.[5] But he was not consistent; and Luther was not impressed. 'Should I not call my Lord Jesus Christ by a name which is not in scripture? There is no name in scripture which would comprise all sacraments or signs' (WA, XVIII, 141, 11 sq.). He knew that scriptural language as such is no safeguard against heresy, and he goes on to argue:

[1] The reply of the Bishops of the Church of Sweden to the Conference of Bishops in the Anglican Communion, cf. Bell, *Documents of Christian Unity*, I, 189 sq.

[2] See O. Ritschl, op. cit. II, 253.

[3] 'Sed iuniores moneo, ut fontes rerum recte discant, et sint circumspecti in loquendo, et retineant formas receptas gravi autoritate. Quia mutatio parit ambiguitates et rixas', *CR*, 24, 133.

[4] 'Was die alten christlichen Lehrer gehalten', *CR*, 7, 216; *Interim Cellense*.

[5] See Elert, op. cit. I, 163 sq.

'In sensu, non in verbis est haeresis...alioqui maximus sit haereticus Moses, qui decalogum ipsum diversa forma recitat Exod. xx
et Deut. v...tanta est simplicitas et bonitas spiritus sancti, ut
homines sui, dum falsa loquuntur (grammatice) vera loquuntur
sensu; tanta est versutia et malitia sathanae, ut homines sui, dum
vera loquuntur (grammatice, id est verbis) mendacia loquuntur....
Hoc est, quod dicitur haereticum esse, qui scripturas aliter intel-
ligit, quam flagitat spiritus sanctus.'[1]

Ambiguity and fallibility are, however, not the fault of scripture but of the heretic. That is the other side of the truth that
'in sensu, non in verbis est haeresis', and Melanchthon is as clear
about it as Luther. 'Sed quid si sit ambiguitas? Hic primum
respondeo: Non est ambiguitas in fundamento, in partibus necessariis, in libris propheticis, apostolicis et symbolis, dextre con-
sideratis sententiis sine sophistica, et collato integro doctrinae
corpore.'[2] The 'synagogue' (see above, p. 91) has erred, not
the Church; the Councils and Popes, not the Word of God
(CR, 15, 1345 sqq.). To hunt for contradictions in scripture is
always the mark of disobedience;[3] heresy consists in 'Eigen-
sinnigkeit',[4] whereas 'catholicity' is consent to, and contentment
with, the all-sufficient source of revelation, whose lucidity is
reflected and confirmed by the witness of the early church.[5]
In the words of the Collect for the Third Sunday after Easter:
it is 'the light of thy truth' which makes us return from error
'into the way of righteousness' so that we 'are admitted into the
fellowship of Christ's religion'; that return implies 'that they
may eschew those things that are contrary to their profession,
and follow all such things as are agreeable to the same'. The
boundaries of scripture are not narrow; there is ample scope for
variety in 'all such things as are agreeable to the same'; the only
condition imposed upon us by the Apostle is 'not to think above

[1] Disp. Drews, p. 589, Th. 57–64.
[2] CR, 15, 1349; see above, p. 13, note 4.
[3] 'Multi autem quia non volunt convinci verbo Dei, postea quoque
contradicunt', CR, 15, 1349.
[4] See above, p. 94; and WA, VIII, 389, 24 sq.: 'Catholicus he is called who
is with the whole company and unanimous with them in faith and spirit
(Eph. iv, 4–5). But Haereticus actually means someone who is self-minded
in divine matters, an outsider who knows better and chooses for himself a
way to heaven which the common Christian man does not go (cf. Deut.
xii, 8).'
[5] 'Adiuvamur sinceris testimoniis antiquae Ecclesiae, sicut scriptum est
Lucae 22: Et tu conversus confirma fratres tuos', CR, 15, 1349.

that which is written...not to stretch ourselves beyond our measure...but according to the measure of the rule which God hath distributed to us...that we shall be enlarged by you according to our rule abundantly' (1 Cor. iv, 6; 2 Cor. x, 13 ff.). Within these limits there is room for Matthew and Mark, Luke and John, Paul and James; or, as Luther said, for two (or more) different versions of the decalogue; and there is no harm in the divers interpretations of scripture as long as they correspond to the diversity in scripture itself. This is the final criterion for all Concessions to Diaphora within the Ecumene. Here the Psalm cxxxiii is fulfilled that brethren dwell together in unity; 'qui Psalmus peculiariter de doctrinae concordia concionatur. Quia cum fit mentio balsami, quo Aaron unctus est, doctrina significatur.... Primum igitur ad consensum doctrinae et voluntatum necesse est recte tenere Evangelium' (CR, 15, 336).

But who is to decide whether the sound of any given voice, any particular idiom, in the church is alien or native, belongs to the hireling or to our brother inside the fold? The answer is 'He that heareth you heareth me', and the first classical example of a settled dispute is the Council of Jerusalem in Acts xv (cf. CR, 2, 655; above, p. 12). With typical divergence of approach Melanchthon takes up the defence of Peter in his compromise with the circumcision (Gal. ii, 11 ff.): 'non fuit error doctrinae, sed fuit infirmitas, aut quoquo modo vocandum est; Petrus recte docebat et sentiebat, fuit tamen infirmitas in usu' (24, 950); while Luther, siding with Paul, declares plainly: 'Therefore Peter, with the others, caused real offence, non morum, sed fidei et aeternae damnationis.... It is better that St Peter and St Paul should fall into the sin of unbelief, yes even be anathematized, than that one jot of the Gospel should be corrupted' (WA, 11, 485, 33 sq.). In the ministry, not in the persons of even the Apostles, is the seat of authority. To which Melanchthon agrees: 'Consistit unitas Ecclesiae in hac consociatione sub uno capite per idem Evangelium et idem ministerium, cui debetur obedientia..., ut retineatur unitas fidei et similis usus Sacramentorum et disciplina mandata in Evangelio.'[1]

It is tempting to pursue the parallel between the two Apostles and the two Reformers, though obviously it must not be pressed too far. One would hesitate to call Melanchthon the Peter of Lutheranism and to picture him as the rock upon which the

[1] *Acta Ratisbon* (not in *CR*), De unitate ecclesiae. See also above, pp. 15 sq.

Lutheran Church was built. Yet by virtue of the *Augustana* he ranks as first Confessor; and again, in his manifold 'concessions' there is a resemblance with the conduct of Peter in the Gospels and Acts. What he once said in criticism of the Augsburg Interim is true of all his writings: 'I think, others will not speak so mildly' (*CR*, 6, 845); and in more than one place he falls victim to his own censure: 'the trick, though subtly arranged, is yet found out' (6, 854). The riddle of Melanchthon lies in the disharmony between the concessions and the confessions; and is that not precisely the fate of all of us who, through no choice of their own, are children both of Reformation and Humanism? Where Melanchthon erred in the latter direction, Luther had, and still has, to restore the balance; but not all writings of Luther are canonical either, and it is essential to know that there is room in the one Church for both, as indeed there is for Paul and Peter.[1] 'But if somebody should say: will there then never be an end of dissensions in the Church?' (15, 1350), Melanchthon replies that the Church can never 'settle' its Diaphora by the ways and means of the world; that only by stedfast and patient witness for the truth can the ignorance of foolish men be put to silence (cf. Luke xxi, 15; 1 Pet. ii, 15); and weary from a life-long struggle he comforts himself in a last brief monologue with the prospect of that day when 'discedes a peccatis; liberaberis ab aerumnis et a rabie Theologorum; venies in lucem; videbis Deum; intueberis Filium Dei; disces illa mira arcana, quae in hac vita intelligere non potuisti; cur sic simus conditi, qualis sit copulatio duarum naturarum in Christo'.[2]

[1] Cf. Acts xvi, 3; xxi, 24 sq.; 1 Cor. iii, 12 sq.; xii, 22 sq.; 2 Tim. ii, 20.
[2] *CR*, 9, 1098: 'Caussae cur minus abhorreas a morte, scriptae a Phil. Melanchthone in pagella, paucis diebus ante obitum.'